A Far Cry from Sunset

Billy Franks

Copyright © 2012 Billy Franks
All rights reserved

ISBN-13: 978-1479340903

ISBN-10: 1479340901

Published By - The B-Spot.
We Know Where It's At

A DEDICATION

For Jim

CONTENTS

1	The Girl of Your Dreams	9
2	Just	19
3	The Sacred Art of Leaving	37
4	Love Being Lost	61
5	This Evil Man	69
6	Sing It One More Time for the Broken-Hearted	85
7	I Wanna Be Your Country	103
8	Sleep A Little Easy When It Rains	119
9	Alone With What You Know	135
10	The Strange Story of Myself	151

Acknowledgments

To my wonderful family and friends who guided me from the blank page to the final draft.

To my long-time loyal supporters who never gave up on me.

To Christopher Brookmyre who always leads by example.

And to my three fellow travellers: Mick McCleery, Mike Nicholson and Gary Joseph, who didn't only take me on a sun- lit journey, but helped me make this book shine.

My love and my gratitude to you all.

Billy

The Key Arena - Seattle - 11pm

The black sedan roared up the ramp towards the security gates. Two heavyweight guards stood, one on each side, ready to open and close the gates as soon as the car hit the street. We could see the license plate - Seattle20. It was the same car we had kept tabs on all day after a naive stagehand had let slip that this was the car our man had arrived in earlier.

Flipping open his phone, Mike called our two friends who were sitting in a rented car halfway down the street opposite the stadium gates.

"He's leaving. The car he came in. It's leaving now!"

While Mike and I didn't want to miss out on the drama, the car and its quarry would soon dissolve into the night if our friends waited too long for us. We tore up the street. Gary and Mick were sitting up front, the engine running. I still had one leg half out of the open back door when we screeched away from the curb.

Seattle20 took a left and, for a brief moment, disappeared from sight. As we turned the corner, there they were, sitting at a red light at the top of the hill road. The car slowed down, but my heart was thumping hard and fast.

"He's definitely in there!" I said. He was running towards the car's open door, and he was bent over with a baseball cap covering his face, but I could still tell it was him.

We followed slowly for a while. Then, at another red light, traffic forced us to pull up alongside. The sedan's windows were as black as its cat-like, sleek body. From the deep purring of the engine, it was clear this car could easily outrun us. We sank low in our seats, but Gary continued to film slyly from the half open passenger window. If he was spotted, the chase was over. But when you're making a guerrilla-style documentary feature film involving some of the biggest names in rock music, this kind of footage is pure gold.

We had planned to discreetly follow the car to our man's chosen hotel and then, should his personal security leave him alone for even a few seconds, well...we would move on him.

Like a panther, the sedan suddenly leapt into gear and tore away from the red light. They had seen us.

We tried to catch up but it wasn't easy. The driver was well skilled, pulling every car chase trick: flashing his turn signal, but not turning; slowing for a red light, then speeding through and leaving us stuck there; throwing us into wrong turns at crossroads. Now we were edgy with fear and excitement. If the police were called, it would wreck everything, but the thrill of the chase had gotten under our skin.

Catching up with these guys was like trying to catch an elusive animal familiar with its own dark territory. We caught up, and then lost them again for a few precious seconds. We again picked up the trail as the sedan zigzagged through the empty streets of downtown Seattle at top speed. We soon realized we were seeing the same buildings over and again. We were no longer following; we were hunting. This wasn't how it should go. This was never part of the plan. Just yards ahead was the man we had travelled thousands of miles to find. What if we never got this close again? It was time for a tough decision - keep up the chase, or show respect and stand down? We had been watching those security gates all day. We had seen four people climb into Seattle20 - the driver and bodyguard in the front seats, and a tall red headed woman in the back. Behind the driver slipped our famous target - Bruce Springsteen. We had to decide, and quickly.

BILLY FRANKS

A FAR CRY FROM SUNSET

Introduction

Starting in the summer of 2005, three friends and I took an eight month journey across the two continents of America and Europe.

We were on a mission: to get 10 of the world's most famous recording artists to record a tribute album to an unknown songwriter. That songwriter would be me.

As we travelled, we were going to make a road movie, an epic chronicle of our quest, and a testament to our friendship.

We made it and called it, *Tribute This!*

The adventures we had and the people we met changed my life profoundly. Not only its present but also how I view its past.

Apart from our struggles with managers, publicists, security, and even one or two of the artists themselves, we ran into so many people from ordinary walks of life: cab drivers, hotel porters and fans standing in line to see their heroes, who couldn't do enough to help or encourage us on our journey.

For one long summer, we lived life so brilliantly, so full of laughter and a gathering sense of achievement, that I wondered if the artists we were pursuing ever got to see life in anything like the same way.

In contrast, they seemed so protected, so hidden away, so cut off from the world that, towards the end of our travels, the thought occurred to me, at that point in time, I wouldn't swap one year of their lives for one day of ours.

My hope is, in reading my account of those heady days, along with the memories from my musical life, you will understand why.

Billy Franks

"Our battered suitcases were piled on the sidewalk again; we had longer ways to go. But no matter, the road is life." – Jack Kerouac

BILLY FRANKS

1. The Girl of Your Dreams

You're looking at a man whose dreams didn't come true.

These are dreams I've had since I was a boy, for so long in fact, I can't remember a time without them. Truth is, in my pursuit of them, I hadn't really been looking where I was going; too busy hunched over a guitar, a piano, or a notebook to plot anything like a straight course.

How do I feel about it? It depends when you ask me. Ask me when I have just read a T. S. Eliot poem, from a collection that sold only three thousand copies, and I feel I can live with it. Put the same question to me when I've just heard some vapid pop cat or kitten complaining about the workload, and I don't know whether to arm myself for a slaughter, or just break down and cry.

You're looking at a man whose dreams didn't come true.

The thought first pounced on me late one night while nursing a large brandy in The Troubadour Club in

London. My band and I had just finished our final set of the night.

There were a handful of us sitting around talking, and this guy suddenly asked me a question I had been asked so many times before: how had I been able to keep going for so long, despite remarkably little real success. My usual answer is that I am in love with what I do, and it has never been a question of persevering or quitting. This is what I do, and this is who I am. From a stage made of milk crates in a slum yard to opening for U2 in front of 63,000 people at Milton Keynes Bowl, it has never occurred to me to imagine any other life.

You're looking at a man whose dreams didn't come true.

The thought wounded me. Not that it had taken me by surprise, (I had sensed it lurking in a dark corner of my mind for some time), but I was shaken by its ferocity and I couldn't bring myself to utter it. It was as if by releasing it into the world, its presence in my life would make it only more vicious. Falling into bed a few hours later, I was moved to write it down, but again it lashed out, and I put pen and paper aside and let it go.

In the summer of 2005, three friends took me on an insane quest that would change my chosen world, my dreams, and the way in which I would come to reflect upon them. The quest was to ask 10 world famous singers to record a tribute album to an unknown songwriter. The unknown songwriter was to be me.

The idea had first come to us the summer before. We were sitting in a New Jersey bar and I was holding court with yet another story of a lost opportunity: I had been offered a slot on a tribute album to Bruce Springsteen by a Spanish music magazine. (A friend of mine ran the Boss's UK fan club and had pulled in a favor). I had chosen my contribution, the beautiful, *Stolen Car*, from his album, *The River*. I had even started recording it when word came back that a big name had jumped in and I, being of little name, had been bounced out. My friends cursed and ordered me another brandy. I told them it was no big deal.

"And anyway", I joked, "I have decided I'm going to get a bunch of famous artists to make a tribute album to me!"

We laughed, but when the laughter faded, Mick said:

"You know what? You should do it! The journey to get that tribute album made would make a great road movie. We could travel around, try to talk to some famous artists, in a guerrilla style, into being on that album, and document the quest."

He even came up with a title there and then: *Tribute This!*

A great idea always sounds different to me. I have ideas running through my mind through the waking hours of most days. The ordinary ones sound the same as each other, but the truly great ones leave a note as they pass by. Like a finger ran round the edge of a fine-cut glass; it is a sound that's hard to imitate, and it whistles up my sense of adventure. A wine connoisseur will tell you that he can, simply from the aroma, tell the grape, the region and the vintage. When I get a whiff of adventure, I can taste the excitement, I can sense the voyage, and I know I am about to make the most of my time. When Mick popped open that idea, I heard that rare and welcome ring.

Mick had been making films since he was eight years old, and I had played the lead role in a couple of them. He is a class act, and I had long believed that all he needed was a film, or an idea, that would grab industry attention and bundle him into the spotlight. I believed this was it. The rest of us looked at him and I made a rather clumsy but heartfelt speech about remembering this moment as we were considering an adventure that could change all of our lives.

We talked of nothing else until the bar lights went out. We didn't want to make a film that was no more than a self-serving publicity stunt; we wanted a film that would capture the quality of our friendship and the relentless nature of our humor.

Nobody can beat a gag to death as we do. It was also important that the artists we eventually chose were approached with at least a little respect. Mick came up with a way to shoot. Like gunslingers, each of us would be armed with a hand held camcorder ready to be drawn at the first sign of any action. A high end camera would be unpacked when we came face-to-face with a big shot.

Artist security would be our biggest problem but I couldn't imagine we would be easily bullied out of any situation. Mick's a big guy. Gary and I aren't small, but he dwarfs us. He has a tough but handsome face and a full head of black hair. He's quite a presence. Yet I have only ever seen him stop a fight, never get drawn into one.

A FAR CRY FROM SUNSET

I guess anyone looking for trouble wouldn't look for it in his direction.

Mick and I had become friends after he spent a semester in London back in 1989. I was playing every Saturday at a bar just down the road from where he was staying, and Mick and his friends would come along each week to catch us play. He was already a budding film maker and was shooting a travelogue of his six months in England. He filmed one of our shows and a few days later we met and swapped tapes. He gave me a VHS of the gig and I gave him a cassette of a dozen songs of mine.

From then on, I would spend my summers over in New Jersey making pop videos and independent thrillers. Gary was part of the team, and the funniest guy I had ever met. He had a shaven head and a goatee. Not an uncommon look but because of his warm and relentless humor, Gary gave that look a softer, kinder rounding. He was as kind as he was funny. More than once Gary has bailed me out during hard times.

More than any group of people I had ever known, these guys got things done. If one of us had an idea in the morning, we would shoot that day and probably edit that night. I have always liked to work that way myself and felt I had found like-minded souls. Mike joined the crew a few years later and had exactly the same flair and fire. If Mick dwarfed Gary and me, then we both got a little back on Mike, who was the shortest of the four of us. This earned him the nickname "Baby Legs", a moniker Gary had come up with when he noticed Mike's legs never quite reached the plane seat in front of him when we traveled. His small round glasses gave him an air of intelligence that was well deserved. Mike taught English along with film and video at a local high school, and his knowledge of literature in particular gifted him and me with many evening-long conversations.

Mike is also morally tight. He'll take any of us to task to be sure we are doing the right thing. But whatever we set our hearts on doing, we not only got it done, we laughed our way through doing it. The four of us became inseparable. We now had a task that would put all of our combined qualities to the toughest of tests.

While Mick, Gary and Mike looked at the schedules of some famous acts, I returned to London to try and raise some cash. My plan was to talk to 10 of my less than destitute friends and ask them to invest, particularly those who knew my work and might be willing to back the film for a cut of its profits. They would each be asked to sponsor one of the 10 songs we planned to feature in the film. First stop, The Troubadour and an Irish coffee with my dear friend, Simon Thornhill, who owns and runs what is my favorite bar in the city. I ran through the premise and told him the outline of our plans. Gary had created a movie poster, based on an idea from Mick, that remains the same to this day, and as soon as I rolled it out for Simon, he bankrolled himself in.

It was always going to be tough to persuade famous faces to record a tribute album to an unknown songwriter, but it might be easier if the proceeds from that record went to a worthwhile charity.

A FAR CRY FROM SUNSET

So we promised any money made from the album would go to *Youth Music* which raises money to buy instruments for inner city kids who could not otherwise afford them.

With the charity on board and our first five grand in the bank, we selected around 20 artists who at least one or two of us respected. We favored those who would be on the road that summer, and plotted our course. It was going to be an epic trail that over the entire summer would, by air, rail and road, lead us to our chosen final 10.

Mick had come up with another hard and fast rule for the movie: no two artists would be approached in the same way. Each assignment, from the dangerous to the cute, would be unique. So while I was still in London drumming up funds, the guys had devised a mission that would make for a perfect test run. Not only would the three of them make the first proposal to a chosen artist, they would do so live on national television. In doing so, we would announce, in a small and subtle way, the commencement of our quest to the nation. They were driving from their home town of Philadelphia to New York where the plan was to get the message to Huey Lewis. Huey and The News were performing at Bryant Park for ABC Television's *Good Morning America,* and it was being broadcast live on TV and online.

I watched on my laptop from the comfort of my sofa. I didn't mind not seeing Huey Lewis.

It struck me, as I watched, that travelling the world to watch these big names, a few of whom had been inspirational to me while I was learning to do my thing, play for massive audiences, was not going to be easy for me. It never has been. They live the life I have dreamed of since I was a kid. I have often described it as seeing the love of your life in the arms of another guy. Ironically, the song of mine chosen for Huey was called *The Girl of Your Dreams.*

Gary, his shaven head all shiny under the TV lights, had been interviewed as an audience member by ABC News as the crowd was gathering, so things looked good. As the park filled, I saw in the corner of my screen Huey Lewis heading towards the stage. A cheer rose from the crowd and, as I swigged from my mug of tea, I noticed my friends, using Mick's hulking frame as the cutting edge, plough their way through the crowd to the front. As Huey lumbered into the first song, the guys popped open three large, grey umbrellas. Across them in bold black letters, there was a message. The crowd, seeing the message before I did, let out an enormous roar of approval.

The news cameras zoomed in on them. There, for all of America to see, were scrawled the words: *Huey! A Tribute Album to an Unknown Songwriter. For A Kid's Music Charity! Say Yes! Tributethis.com!*

Huey Lewis looked horrified. The three of them were immediately set upon by security and ejected from the park. I laughed out loud. An adventure was underway, and I wanted desperately to take my part in it.

A FAR CRY FROM SUNSET

The Girl of Your Dreams

(Scan QR code to download song)

BILLY FRANKS

A FAR CRY FROM SUNSET

2. Just

I was at Bruce Springsteen's concert in Wembley Stadium, London in June 1985.

Before he covered the Elvis Presley classic, *Falling in Love with You*, he told this story.

"It was 1976, the Born to Run Tour. We played in Memphis one night. We came home after the show, and me and my guitar player, Steve, were sitting around, and we called a taxi cab to come and take us out to Elvis's house.

So the cab driver came, and he brought us out to Graceland.

I got out of the cab and stood in front of those gates with the big guitar players on them. Me and Steve were standing there, and I saw a light on in a second story window. So I figured Elvis must be up reading or something!

I jumped up over the wall and down onto the other side and started running up the driveway as fast as I could. I ran right up to the front door and was about to knock when a guard came out of the woods and asked me what I wanted.

I said, "Well, is Elvis home?"

He said no, Elvis isn't home tonight, he's in Lake Tahoe. I tried to tell him, "well, I'm a guitar player too, and I got my own band....". He looked at me like I was crazy; I don't think he believed me.

I never got to meet him.
You know, it's easy to let the best of yourself slip away. So I'd like to do this song for you tonight, wishing you all the very best of everything you can get your hands on."

♦

I was now reunited with my friends and we were flying from Philadelphia to Seattle to catch Bruce at The Key Arena. I remembered his Elvis story and recounted it to them. We couldn't help but feel there was a kind red spirit between his tale and our own.

There are two music giants I spent my formative years straining my neck to look up to. One is Paul McCartney. He is songwriting's definitive craftsman. Writing a song is like trying to open a safe. You struggle to find an order for the ideas tumbling in your head. You find the right combination, the lock drops and *voila*! The door opens.

A FAR CRY FROM SUNSET

Now you can help yourself to the shiny stuff. Well McCartney is a safe cracker par excellence.

The other was Bruce Springsteen. I was loaned a copy of *Born to Run* while we were recording demos for our first band, Scruff. The American guy who was producing the songs, Wally Brill, handed it to me, telling me this was something he thought I needed.

The Boss came along when I was young and punk rock was the zeitgeist. I liked a lot of it, but I have an instinctive mistrust of anger. In song, no less than in conversation, it can make you spiteful.

The Punk promise was of no fun and no future, but from my shared bedroom on a rough council estate in south London, I was looking for somewhere to go and someone to be. *Born to Run* blew the doors right off. I was hurled into a world where restless hearts like my own could either stay and fight, or make a run for it and find a world big enough to hold them. *Born to Run* is to an open mind what a Harley Davidson is to an open road. Its songs roared through me and blew my soul away. It made me want whatever there was to be earned, found or just taken.

My first band, Scruff, had started when my closest friend, Lee and I were walking back from The Castle Youth Club in our home borough of Fulham. I told him I could play the guitar, that I desperately wanted to be in a band, and that I could at least teach him rudimentary bass – maybe we could start something ourselves? We both had similar build and long hair to the shoulders. His blonde and mine brown. This already distinguished us from the shaven headed kids that made up most of our age group in the council estate we lived in. Being in a band together would set us apart just a little more. A prospect as dangerous as it was exciting.

Fulham has a vibrant bustling market called North End Road with stalls and barrows on one side and high street shops on the other. Just where the market ended was an electrical junk-yard of a shop called Olympic Radio. It was from here that I bought my first electric guitar. I was 14 when it first caught my eye, and I was smitten. The kindly old geezer who ran the shop saw me gazing longingly through the window for the third afternoon in a row, the price tag teasing me at £8. He came outside, pushed his glasses up into his thinning grey hair, and talked to me as if the six-string was his girl and I was about to take a risk by asking her to dance.

"If you want my girl that badly, you should come to the shop every time you have spare pocket money. I will keep the payments logged in a little red book until you have paid me what she's worth. Then, I'll hand her over to you. Until then, I'll look after her and nobody else will get a look in."

For the next three months I ran paper rounds, door stepped milk bottles for local milkmen, even worked on a couple of stalls in the market itself. Anything that would help me take that beauty home. When I finally settled up, we dressed her in carrier bags and I took her home to meet the family.

Up until then, I had taught myself on an acoustic guitar that was coming apart at the seams so badly that the strings were a good inch from the fret board. It would make my fingers bleed. The new girl wasn't quite so rough, but I had no amp, so unless you put your ear to the wood, you could hardly hear a note she sang.

Lee and I had grown up in Fulham Court. A sprawling council estate tucked away between Fulham Broadway and Putney Bridge. Almost directly opposite was the ABC cinema. On an almost weekly basis, we would bunk in and watch the latest films, from Disney to Deep Throat.

By the time we reached our late teens and started our first band, the place had been bought by progressive rock gods, *ELP*, renamed The Manticore, and hired out to famous bands to rehearse before major tours. Coming from poor families and having no income of our own, it seemed only fair that we should use the many ways into the building that we knew, and help ourselves to an amp or two from bands who could easily afford to replace them. Pretty soon my bedroom was well stocked with high end band tackle. But bands have a habit of stenciling their name in big bold white letters on everything they own. This made my mother a little suspicious. I eased her worries by convincing her we were simply changing our band name on a regular basis until we could settle on one that we liked. In response she said:

"Well then, what kind of a name is *Led Zeppelin*?! You should have stuck with *Status Quo*; it had a nice ring to it!"

Lee's brother, Mark, had bought him his first bass from Woolworths. We practiced for a while with what we had, but neither guitar was good enough to leave the house with. Fortunately for us, The Hammersmith Odeon was another place we knew multiple routes into. On the night *10cc* played there, Lee and I stole in over the roof, popped a window, and clambered down through the venue until we ended up in the orchestra pit, convincing security we were the sons of the band's official photographer.

When the gig was over, we wedged the fire exit door open with some cardboard, and went in search of a bag of chips. Bellies full, we came back an hour later, removed the wedge, and, with security on the stage only yards away, broke open the door to the band dressing room. We had actually tried the support act's dressing room first, (the cockney duo, *Chas & Dave*) but seeing they had only two guitars, we didn't have the heart to take them. By comparison, in *10cc*'s room, the guitars were piled high. 11 in all, I think. With alarming audacity, we locked the door, drew the curtains, turned on the light, and tried out every guitar in the stack until we found a pair we liked. Loaded up, we headed back down the fire escape and the long, clandestine route home along the river by Putney tow path.

The next day it was all over the radio, and the gossip around Fulham Court was that it had to have been the two of us. The story even featured in a cartoon strip in the following month's *Jackie Magazine*. The funny twist in this tale is that only a couple of years later Steve Jones, guitarist of *The Sex Pistols*, publicly took credit for *our* heist.

A FAR CRY FROM SUNSET

With stolen guitars to plug into our stolen amplifiers, all we needed now were stolen drums. But drummers tend to tidy their kit away, and besides, drums are awkward to illegally leave a building with. Luckily, I had a girlfriend who worked at a local dry cleaner who had unwisely told me that the manager always left the week's takings in the shop over the weekend.

The next Sunday afternoon, Lee, myself, and another guy from our band, climbed into the shop's backyard and took down the door. Inside we found over 200 quid. A fair amount now, a fortune then.

So back in my bedroom we were counting it out for our needs:

"Bass Drum…..sixty quid!"
"Snare Drum …… …. forty!"
"Hi Hat………..thirty five!"

My mum, who must have been listening at the door, popped her head in and said:

"Billy boy, come out here, I want to talk to you."
Sounded like trouble.

"Listen, Billy" she said, "I don't know what you get up to and I don't care what you get up to…
…but you have to cut me in!"
So I dropped her 20 quid, and off she went to bingo.

Throughout her life my mother's only real escape from hardship was the bingo hall. There she would meet with friends for the cheap afternoon tea sessions on the odd evening she could afford. When she won, there was always a treat in it for us kids. When we were still very young she had once, after copping a full-house, bought my brother Jim and me Beatles suits - the ones with the black velvet collars. They were pretty cheap, and the material so thin you could almost see through it. Even so, she was adamant we could only wear them for special occasions, so Jim and I started going to church every Sunday. We may have had to sing *Onward Christian Soldiers* but it felt like *She Loves You*. Pretty soon, the suits fell apart, and Jim and I fell from grace.

The next evening, Lee and I were bashing around on the newly acquired kit.

"Who shall we get to play em," asked Lee.
"Mmmm," I said, "let me see who's in the front room."

On the other side of my bedroom wall, my brother, Jim and Mum's new boyfriend, Ken, were watching the American crime series, Longstreet, in which the central character, the detective, was blind.

"Jim, what are you up to?"
"I'm watching Longstreet, why?"
"We're looking for a drummer for our band."
"Oh, alright then," he said, and left Longstreet fumbling around for clues.

Back in the bedroom with Jim at the kit, we were trying to work out what we were supposed to do now.

"I think, as you're the drummer, Jim, you're supposed to count us in."

A FAR CRY FROM SUNSET

"Ok," he says, "after 10, everybody in!"

Over the coming months, we put together a four piece band that wasn't altogether bad. Jim was, by now, a pretty decent drummer, and another guy from our neighborhood, Vince, was on lead guitar.

Scruff started out, as most young bands do, progressing from youth clubs, through working men's clubs, to bars and proper venues. Unlike most bands, though, even when we were playing the hot-spots of south London, we were still carting our gear from gig to gig on a wheelchair. All of it. Piled seven feet high. What made it worse was that the left wheel was buckled so the chair dipped on every turn, meaning all four of us had to hold the gear in place at the corners as we tramped the streets of our hometown.

Early one evening as we were bouncing the gear along North End Road, we passed the very theatre from which we had stolen our amps only months before. As we trundled by, *Blue Oyster Cult*'s road crew were loading their band's equipment into the venue. They had three *Edwin Shirley* trucks, ramps, forklifts, the works. One guy spots us and calls about a dozen others out to catch the spectacle. At the sight of them pointing with one hand and holding their quivering fat guts with the other, our guitar player, Vince, got embarrassed and let go of his corner. With that, all our gear hit the street, some of it falling apart on impact. This sent the *Cult*'s road crew into hysterics. We piled our gear's splintered remains onto our three-wheeled chair and skulked off home.

Later that night, still seething from the shame of it all, I was talking to my brother, Jim, telling him how it hurt that another band's crew had ridiculed us publicly. We needed to step up.

"It's no good," I said. "I can't go on like this, something has to change, it's just embarrassing."
"I know," says Jim. "We're gonna have to get a new wheelchair."

♦

In Seattle, Mick, Gary, Mike and I were looking for a break at the venue Bruce was playing. We asked around, but no one was giving too much away. We learned that Bruce was already inside, and wouldn't be coming out till after the show.

At one point, I climbed a wall and tried to make my way into the venue, but I got caught by a security guard. It was a faint echo of the story I had heard at Wembley Stadium all those years before.

We hung around until after the show, and managed to find out from a stage-hand that Bruce was travelling in a hired car with Seattle20 on the license plate.

Could we follow the car back to where Bruce was staying? Maybe join him for a nightcap at the bar and tell him about our quest?

Mick and Gary will wait in our car for when he drives by. Mike and I will keep close eyes on the back gate where the artists usually exit from. We will phone them if we see Bruce leave, and they can follow where he goes. If they have to leave us stranded here, so be it. After about half an hour, from some distance away, I spot Bruce and his wife, Patti, jumping into a saloon. We alert the other two by phone, and not wanting to miss the action, run like hell to join them before Seattle20 speeds past. They have the engine running and the doors open. We jump in. We catch sight of the limo and gently follow a fair way behind. After a mile or so, we pull up alongside them at a light, but can see nothing through the tinted windows. Suddenly, Bruce's driver has realized we are following them, and things get crazy. He pulls off all kinds of manoeuvres - indicating but not taking turns, slowing for a light before speeding through. Mick is at the wheel and trying desperately to keep up, but he's up against a professional. Gary is ducked down in the passenger seat trying to capture the chase on camera. Mike and I are in the back alternately excited and concerned. We seem to be driving in circles. When we pass our own hotel for the third time, it's clear they are trying to give us the slip.

Then it hits us. We hate this kind of behavior. Chasing someone we respect like ruthless paparazzi makes us feel like creeps. So we make the decision to back down.

"Our problem in taking on this task is we're really not cut out for it," says Mick. "Maybe it's not the job for us."
"We're too nice," adds Mike.

They are right. It isn't the ethic we wanted to travel with, so we head back to the hotel for a Bruce-less nightcap and a rethink.

We weren't looking to stalk these people. This is not one of those deals where some half-wit bugs a celebrity and makes fools of them both. This was from the heart. My friends wanted to talk to the elder statesmen of the songwriting fraternity with the respect they deserved, and ask them if they would give a hand up to a "disinherited brother" I have a small but loyal following that helps keep me alive year after year, but sometimes it's tough simply getting by. You could probably fit all the Billy Franks fans in the world on one tube train. Fellow travellers might include three bestselling novelists, a member of the British Royal Family, and the lead singer with the world's biggest rock outfit, but even so, everyone would get a seat.

I was struggling, and my friends wanted to help.

After the realization from the Springsteen car chase, we had a few drinks and concluded that, as determined as we would remain, we would keep our attempts at getting to artists a fairway short of a hounding. The following morning, we started the long drive to Vancouver where Springsteen had another show.

What pulls this crew through anything is its synergy. We are each at our best when we are all together. When one of us is missing, it's like a wheel has come off our bandwagon. It's only when all four of us are hitched up that we roll as fast and as funny; never more so than when on long journeys.

When we get to the Canadian border we see the unbelievable sight of a house half on the US side, half over in Canada.

"You think they got immigration in that house," I say.

A FAR CRY FROM SUNSET

"They'd have to, surely?"
"Yeah", imagines Gary, "a guy sits there on a stool."
"You get up at night to go to the bathroom," says Mick
"Take off your belt, shoes and jacket, put all your little things in that tray," I add.

Gary imitates an officer: "Hey buddy, where do ya think you're going? Got anything to declare?"
Mick snatches the punch- line: "Yeah, I gotta take a shit!"

We found a hotel, dumped our things in the rooms, and made for the bar. There's an old fella singing there, and I swear he sounded exactly like Bruce. His rendition of *I'm on Fire* sounded so much like the Boss that we called the guy over during his break to tell him so. He's a sweetheart and we made him a promise that if Bruce turns us down, he could take his slot on the tribute album. He loved it and laughed.

In the afternoon, we headed out to the GM Place for another shot at Springsteen. The guard back in Seattle had told us that Bruce regularly takes a few minutes to talk to fans on his way into a gig, so early afternoon would be the perfect time to grab a minute with him.

There's a small problem. Another artist we're after, Aaron Neville, is playing the same town on the same night. We'd have to split into pairs. Lots were drawn and I wouldn't be half of the duo that would get to talk to Bruce. So while Mike and Gary went to ask Bruce to be on the album, Mick and I made for the festival where the Neville Brothers were making an appearance.

The song we had chosen for Aaron was *Love Being Lost*, a song I wrote when, having no place to call my own, I spent several years travelling around the US. Travelling with a guitar and more songs than clothes will get you through a lot of sympathetic doors. It can reveal the common nature of everyday human kindness.

A few years before, I was living in Austin, Texas. I had gone for a 10 day music convention and fell in love with the place, and so I took up the offer from a girl I had met to stay on a while. After a few weeks, I was broke. I was in the small local store trying to send postcards to both my young daughters. It turns out I only had enough money left for one international stamp. The elderly lady, Rose, who ran the shop, cottoned on to my problem and asked how come. I told her I had been living there for a couple of months and had finally run out of cash. She offered to lend me $50 dollars, with the stipulation that I only paid it back if, and when I could afford it. Her generosity not only solved this and other problems, but took my breath away. I had visited the store once or twice before but we had not exchanged more than a few pleasantries. Yet, she was happy to stump up 50 of her hard earned dollars to bail out someone she may never see again. A month later, I got a gig at the University of Texas, and put the 50 bucks in with a thank you card. Rose and I remained friends for over a decade until she passed away a few years ago.

I loved that time in my life. Never sure where I would end up or who with; each day started as a mystery.

A FAR CRY FROM SUNSET

♦

The festival where the Neville Brothers were playing was well-guarded. We had to sneak our cameras in, and though some backstage workers made promises to tell Aaron we were at the gate wanting to talk with him, it was just a lot of waiting around and wandering.

Back outside the GM Place, Gary and Mike had been standing around for hours, too. The crowd waiting for a glimpse of Bruce was growing ever bigger.

Somehow, Mike and Gary managed to keep their place right on the barrier. Just when their hope started to falter, Bruce's head of security came over and told them Bruce will be here in a few minutes and he'll come by and sign stuff. It's that one shot time.

At the festival, a crew member approaches us and asks Mick for a card. Turns out that a film maker friend of Mick's had worked with The Neville Brothers before and hopefully that puts us a step closer. We wait by the gate for another hour or so, but there's no sign of Aaron.

The crowd at the GM Place starts buzzing. A tinted windowed van has stopped nearby, and the Boss has just stepped out.

Mick and I try the side of the festival stage area and spot Aaron about to walk out to perform. We shout, but he's too far away to notice. We find a gap in the fence and slip through. Aaron is on the ramp that leads to the stage. We have seconds before he makes his entrance. We make a run for the ramp and are immediately blocked by two huge security guards. We shout again, but now we look like stalkers, and the game is up.

Meanwhile Bruce is working the line; signing albums and posters and inching his way towards Gary and Mike.

The Nevilles are getting funky and Mick and I are getting pissed off. Our chance has gone. We call the others in the hope they have better news. They are thrilled. They got their man. Over the phone they fill us in.

As Bruce got to them, Gary handed Bruce the *Tribute This!* Poster; he took a long look and laughed. (Well, his picture, along with the other nine artists, is on it.)

"Hey, Bruce, you ever thought about doing a tribute album?"
"Thought about it." Bruce replied.
"Ever thought about doing a tribute album to an unknown songwriter, Bruce?"
"That's great", said Bruce.

Bruce, not really wanting to be drawn, is still laughing and signing our poster.

"His name is Billy Franks!"
"Never heard of him." said Bruce.
"Oh he's a great songwriter. He's from London. We're raising money for the Youth Music charity."

Bruce is moving on.
Gary, never one to let go easily, shouts, "Bruce, we'll be in touch!"

A FAR CRY FROM SUNSET

It's a good shout because just after he gently guided Bruce away, the head of security took Gary to one side and took our details. He also told us where to send our formal request. Compared to our earlier efforts, this is a success.

We knew this much from the outset: nobody in our line of fire is gonna sign up for such a project in a hotel bar or outside a sound-check, but making a road movie from footage of conference calls is beyond even the greatest directors.

Gary and Mike came and joined Mick and I at the festival and we had a few celebratory beers. We were just about to quit when Aaron Neville broke into his version of Sam Cooke's masterpiece, *A Change is Gonna Come*. Now it's a beautiful song when Sam does it, but when Aaron puts that sweet, quivering soul into it, I could break down and weep. The thought of that voice singing *Love Being Lost* sends me into dreamland.

But first we had to get back to my homeland. The gentile English town of Oxford. Our quarry; Mike's very own musical hero, Elvis Costello.

Just

(Scan QR code to download song)

3. The Sacred Art of Leaving

My life snaps into focus the night my father leaves for the last time. He makes that camera-clicking sound with the side of his mouth, a kind of verbal wink, and drives off long before I have stopped crying. I watch his blurred back lights dip over Battersea Bridge.

The slum we lived in backed onto the River Thames, and I sat on the steps with the water sloshing at my feet. I felt too ashamed to go back inside. I had left my mother in tears by telling her I wanted to leave with my dad. She had warned me he would turn me down, and she was right, but that wasn't the only reason I couldn't face her. I had chosen him while he had chosen none of us, and even from where I sat, I could hear her heart breaking.

The slum was Battersea Bridge Buildings, and, as bad as it was, it was the first time the five of us had lived under the same roof. I was seven years old. It may have stunk from its intimacy with the river and the river's rats, but we were all together. Mum, Jim, my two younger sisters,

Karen and Dawn, and myself. That we were all together was good enough reason to call it home. It was a single block with inside balconies and outside toilets and held 50 families. A few of those families would move on to Fulham Court with us when the place was eventually pulled down.

The Buildings had its fair share of eccentrics: Ginger Tom, who was always drunk and would ride his bicycle down the inside stairwell to give the kids a laugh; Jimmy Gibbons, whose thick, black, curly hair was always crawling with fleas and who was no taller than Jim and me. He once invited all the kids from the block down to the local department store, *Arding & Hobbs*, to watch him steal a TV. As we stood by the shop's main entrance, Jimmy threw on a white coat, walked into the store, picked up the television of his choice, walked nonchalantly out of the building, and staggered back to the Battersea Bridge Buildings with all the kids laughing and cheering him on.

Before that, we had stayed in an endless string of hostels and half-way houses; some so rotten you daren't sleep at night. My mum and I stayed at a place somewhere on the edge of London that was no more than a corrugated tin shed. There were around 40 beds in there with nothing but sheets hanging to keep them apart. In the corner of the shed lay a woman's dead body for three days before the council came and carried it off. While in another half-way house in Bromley, I was taken to hospital with pneumonia where the head doctor wouldn't check me out for three months because the hole I would return to was so filthy.

A FAR CRY FROM SUNSET

If the wealthy have their names on buildings, the well-off have their names on doors and the poor wear their names on their working clothes. Our names seemed to be on nothing, not sewn into our clothes because all my family wore clothes brought to us by social workers. My name was certainly not on any books because I never went to school. And outside the family almost never on anyone's lips because I spent so much time alone. My name was, though, on a pile of medical files, as I collected every infection and disease poverty was dishing out back then: Scarlet Fever, bronchial pneumonia, dysentery. You name it I had it. By the time I was a young man my constitution was formidable. Even now my body fights back hard against any illness.

My mother smoked heavily. Capstan Full Strength. They came in a brown box with a profile of a bearded sailor on the front. They had no filter and she took such long puffs the cigarettes shrank at the speed of light. Their pulling power was so powerful that if Mum ever ran out she became almost deranged. I remember a morning when she woke us all to help scout the house for lost and hidden coins. We slid under beds, took apart furniture; Jim even ran to our neighbors and asked if he could fleece their couch. One shilling and nine-pence. Somehow we reached the magic number and celebrated like we had broken the record for that year's telethon.

"Billy boy," she said, "run and get me 10 Capstan Full Strength, and be quick."

She was dancing like boys do when they're busting to pee. Now there are at least five tobacconists within 200 yards of us but my first shot was George's. I liked little

Miss George who barely cleared the counter and would always throw in a few extra when you got a quarter bag of sherbet lemons or rhubarb and custard drops.

She looked pleased to see me when I came in panting and jingling like a fruit machine with my pocket full of the nation's smallest coins.

"Ten Capstan Full Strength," I said, almost boastful.
"Sorry Billy, I'm clean out of tens."

"Ok," I said, "gimme a packet of balloons instead." Oblivious to the fact that Mum wanted something to suck in from rather than blow into, I left happy with my purchase and excited to tell the others.

"Miss George didn't have any Capstans so I got these balloons instead" and started blowing into a long yellow beauty.

She cried. I couldn't quite work it out. The balloons were of a great variety. Long ones and round ones in an array of bright colors.

Mum stormed off to her room and Jim, Karen and me started to decorate the living room.

Suddenly we heard laughter. It was coming from Mum's room and growing ever more hysterical. Soon just the sound of her cackling and gasping alternately, gave us the giggles too. When Mum heard us laughing, she started to wheeze before letting out raucous bursts of laughter that the sailor on the absent cigarette pack would have been proud to call his own. By the time she re-entered the gaily balloon-adorned living room. there were tears streaming down her face and us kids collapsed in a bundle shrieking and cackling without really knowing what was so funny.

When it died down a little, in complete innocence, I said, "it looks nice in here don't it?" And Mum went again into another fit of hysterics.

This is the kind of kid I was. I actually did live in a world of my own. Truly there seemed to be nobody else in it. On another shopping errand for my mother, she gave me a pound note telling me to pick up eggs and bread but no party decorations. The old fella that worked behind the counter in the dairy had some awful disease with his hands. They looked like they had once held open a large book and had stuck that way. I picked up the bag of bread and eggs and he gave me first the coins, then the 10 bob note. But as I took the money I noticed not one but two notes, held fast together by their brand spanking newness. For a second or two I was the richest kid in the neighborhood. 10 shillings would have been a day's wages for some men. But I looked at his hands, then his kindly lined face, then back to those buckled hands of his. I couldn't do it. "There are two notes there," I said and my heart bobbed between pride and disappointment. He thanked me and I headed home imagining what I would have done with all that money. How many Capstan Full Strength and balloons could 10 bob could buy?

After dropping the food and change home, I went for a walk around Battersea Park. I was convinced that the universe had a tenner waiting somewhere for me, all I had to do was find it. I looked everywhere for the money owed to me. In the bushes, in the adventure playground, even kicking through every pile of newly swept autumn leaves. After three hours of exhaustive searching all I found was a battered brown park attendant's hat. If there were to be no justice for my kindness to the man at the dairy, it seemed there would be retribution. Mum wanted a smoke and got balloons. I wanted 10 bob and got a weather beaten trilby.

It was around this time that everyone kept inviting God over. Not only were we supposed to worship the fella but we were also impelled to refer to him as Our Father. I've got a father, I would think to myself. Teachers introduced him as merciful while thrashing kids with their weapon of choice. The youth club I went to said between him and the Queen, my time was about to be taken up being forever dutiful to one or the other.

Even my own mother made us swear on the bible whenever anything went missing. I remember a vicar, who we also had to call father, coming to our house, which was filthy, and proclaiming, with complete disdain, that cleanliness was next to godliness. I took one look at my surroundings, took into account that my last bath was a week ago, and promptly decided that both he and God were snobs, and that I would rather wait until my own father came back home to us.

I hadn't yet attended any school, so I was pretty much illiterate. Now that I was enrolled in one, I was so ashamed of what I didn't know that I would often leave home for school in the morning, but spend the day in Battersea Park instead. The school was run by bullies. I remember the headmaster, a stubby ex-military man with greasy silver hair, Mr Newton, rabbit punching me when

A FAR CRY FROM SUNSET

I accidentally got lost between classes. My form teacher, a short and crumpled old bag with a hint of blue to her skin, would rap my knuckles with a ruler while I was writing because I was left-handed. When I wrote with my right hand, it was such a mess that she would hold it up for the class to see and she would lead in the laughter.

Why did teachers back then feel the need to hit you with appropriate weapons? The math teacher with a ruler, the gym teacher with a slipper, and so on. Cruelty at school was such back then that it wouldn't surprise me if the Religious Education teacher kept two planks of wood and a bag of nails tucked away ready for irreverent boys.

I was in the dinner line one lunch time, and, despite my protests, had a lump of cold custard dumped on my plate. I sat at the dinner table and ate everything but the sickly looking yellow slop. The deputy head walked by and told me if I'd taken it, I had to eat it. I refused, and he sent me to the headmaster's office. I had been caned by the head so many times, I was fearful of another, so instead of going to see him I ran home and told my mum what had happened. My mother had been a real beauty in her 20's. Her long wavy brown hair and small features gave her a kind of Mediterranean gypsy look, but she was tough, particularly with anyone who hurt her kids. She put a wrought iron poker in her bag and said,

"We'll see about that."

When we got to the school she said to me:

"You go into his office, and as soon as he gets the cane out, call me, and I'll catch him at it."

43

But I was so afraid of the man that as soon as I shut the door behind me I blurted out:

"Mr Cooke sent me here for not eating all my dinner but my mum's outside with an iron poker in her bag!"

He gave me the meanest look and called me a filthy little coward. At that, my mum burst in and gave him an earful, telling him that if he ever laid another finger on me, she would come back here to beat the living daylights out of him. He left me alone for a while, but I knew he was just waiting for a chance to seek revenge. School became an even more fearful place, and I attended even less than before.

Then the universe finally stepped up; it sent me a sweetheart and I fell in love with music. She arrived at my darkest hour.

Because my mother was bringing the four of us up alone, whenever she was taken into hospital we would be separated again and put into foster care. The place Jim and I were sent to was an avenue of foster homes in Surrey. Each house was run by two adults you had to refer to as uncle and auntie. There were about 10 kids to a house. The auntie of our place was cruel and would often beat us. She was short and fat with red-rash cheeks and black frizzy hair. The uncle was her dead opposite; tall and bony with milk-bottle-bottom glasses. In their cruelty, however, they were an exact match. One summer afternoon, our house was taken to the local park. Our guardians sat among themselves talking and smoking. To keep us kids out of their way, they instructed all of us to run in circles around a huge bush and see who could last the longest. I said it was a stupid idea and wouldn't do it. Auntie warned me I'd get the belt later if I didn't do as I was told, so I ran. I ran in the opposite direction to the others. I ran and wouldn't stop. Even when all the kids had tired and I was running alone, I wouldn't stop. Uncle shouted at me to stop right now and not to be so stupid. I was, he said, "asking for it," but I kept circling that bush till I simply couldn't stand. When we got back to the house, Auntie was as good as her word and I really took a hiding from her. She grabbed me by the arm as soon as we were through the front door, and started to slap me about the head. Next she was whipping right there in the hallway with a wet towel. I was so scared and hurt that I wet myself. That just sent her into a frenzy, and she laid into me with her fists. Eventually, the uncle came and dragged me upstairs by my hair to the dorm room where I would stay in bed the rest of evening.

There was another punished boy three beds away that had an old Dansette record2player at his bedside. He had one song on repeat: *No Reply* by *The Beatles*. I lay there listening in the dark. Suddenly I felt the boy's face right up next to mine in the pitch black, "you tell Auntie about this and I'll fucking kill ya." he said.

You idiot, I thought to myself. If only you knew I was no longer here. No longer in this disturbed house run by child beaters. No longer a poor kid thrown from one lonely hole into another. I was floating through the warm black night, wrapped in sound that seemed to come from out of the void. Comforted by words from a velvet voice that filled, not just the room, but the whole dark and lonely world.

When Jim and I finally got back home, we started a make-believe band. Jim, myself and two other brothers from our block, Ray and Kevin Davey, would build a stage from milk crates at one end of the yard and race down from the other. The order in which you made it to the stage let you decide which Beatle you would be. I was always just fast enough to be either John or Paul.

Jim, bless him, because of his big curly hair and wide eyes was always told to pretend he was Freddie of Freddie and The Dreamers.

♦

I don't know if Mike ever pretended to be Elvis Costello, but he certainly loved him enough to make him one of our chosen artists. That, in turn, made Mike the obvious choice to ask Elvis to take part in our project. The song hooked up for Elvis was *The Sacred Art of Leaving* from my album, *Sex, Laughter & Meditation*. The song came to me one summer afternoon sitting on the balcony of Mick's house. I was thinking about the amount of leaving we have to do through our lives and how we're so lousy at it. If we could somehow manage to leave with some dignity and integrity, not only would we do the honest thing, we would also teach the person we left how to leave decently too. Should they someday have to make that same choice, they would now know how to do it right. Like an art, we would have passed it on.

Back in the UK, we took the train out from London to Oxford. Once again, serendipity played a smart little cameo. Sitting in our carriage talking, we were overheard by an old guy who, it turns out, had a son playing guitar for the opening act at the festival that Elvis Costello was headlining. He gave us his son's number just in case he could help out. I love small world stuff.

On our way to the stately home where the concert was being held, we dropped into a small corner pub for a beer. As we walked in, I noticed that two guys just leaving had festival passes hanging from their necks. With no time to think, I just asked the first question that would stall them.

"You guys working at the festival?"

"Yeah," said the scruffier of the two. I asked him innocently about directions, stage timings and stuff like that until he finally asked what we're going there for. We told him what we were up to and he grinned, wished us the best of luck and he and his pal left. For a moment, I thought we had picked up a real lead.

Mike starts giving us the run-down on how Elvis Costello's songs had almost mirrored his own life.

"What you guys don't get," he said, "is that when I say Elvis has written the soundtrack to my life, I'm deadly serious. Elvis Costello has literally written the soundtrack to my life."

"Ah," says Gary in a fake DJ voice,
"that classic album, Beer, Shitting & Internet Porn."

While we're busy laughing so loud as to disturb the quiet afternoon of the bar's other drinkers, the doors burst open, and in strolled the same two fellas. I guess for some people our madcap quest is just too cute to resist.

"You lot want a lift to the festival? If we get lucky, I might be able to get you right into the production office." We were starting to find this a lot: people we meet from all walks of life offering to do a small favor to help us get along.

"I'm Terry," he said, "I'm working as a production office assistant."

He opened his van doors and we all piled in. Five minutes later, we were in the production house waiting to be called in for a chat with the promoter of the festival. I'm elected to go talk with the promoter. She wasn't having any of it. You can understand; they work hard and pay handsomely to get these stars to appear. They don't want pests like us bugging them all day. We did, though, get four free tickets to the festival as a consolation.

It's your typical small British festival. Beer tents, food stalls selling multicultural snacks, face painted kids, etc. We nosed around to get the run of the place, and it didn't look too tight. Even so, the backstage area was fairly well guarded. It was early afternoon, and since Elvis wasn't performing until later, we sat in the sun with warm beer in plastic cups and tried to come up with a plan. However, we didn't have to. Terry, the guy from the pub, had already devised one. He joined our circle sitting on the grass.

He's going to be at the production house when the convoy leaves to bring Elvis to the backstage area. When the fleet of cars drives through the gates, he will try to usher us inside the gated area to grab a quick word with Elvis, but we'll only get a minute or two before security realizes what's going on, so we will have to be swift and precise. That's not for another few hours, though, so with everything set up, we can enjoy the sun and carnival atmosphere. I have known my three friends for 20 years, but today, for the first time, while we enjoy another beer, they ask me exactly how I got started.

♦

I was 11 years old when my family finally got out of Battersea Bridge Buildings after the place was condemned and brought down. Fulham Court was where they sent us. Fulham Court is hidden away. Its drive-in gate is on a quiet side street, and the main walk-in entrance is a massive grey arch that stands open-mouthed onto Fulham Road. The back of the estate is sealed by the high fencing that guarded the train lines. You didn't stumble into Fulham Court; you either entered or avoided the place with great deliberation. Many times, we watched people cross to the other side of the road rather than pass our archway. It had nine blocks altogether, each of them three stories high with balconies on the outside. Eight of them are back-to-back with a courtyard in between. One, A-Block, is twice the length of the others, and perched over the archway. Always full, the estate housed almost 500 families, some of them big in number and reputation:

The Baxters, from which the oldest son, Kenny, became a life-long friend. His father, John, played trumpet in a big band. John would often invite me to accompany him and his family to band rehearsal. Every week I would request the Glenn Miller songs my mother always loved when I was a kid.

The *Ellis* clan, with eight children in their small second floor flat; nine if you count the cousin, Tony, who was taken under their wing after he had returned from a youth detention centre to find his own family had moved out and on without informing him. Tony was a member of Scruff for a short while before moving on to form his own band, The Caper, and becoming a decent songwriter himself. One of the Ellis family, Sue, a short and curvy blue-eyed blonde, would become my girlfriend for 10 years and the mother of my two daughters, Alison and Billi.

The Kennedys, whose toddler, Lee Kennedy, climbed onto his tricycle and toppled from the second floor balcony into the basement of A-Block to his death. Fulham Court went into an unprompted stillness that day.

Then there was the *Hirons* family, with whom my own family were the closest and from which my good friend, Lee, was one of six kids. His older brother, Mark, hung out with Jim. His two sisters, Joanne and Corrine, were close with my own sisters, Karen and Dawn.

When my own family first moved in, there was a fair bit of fighting to get out of the way before Jim and I could be fully accepted. The new kids always had to be tested by the seasoned fighters so they could be sure their status was safe. There were so many boys around my age that you were kept pretty busy for a while. Some of the better fighters had personal assistants who they would send to your door to make actual appointments to fight you. I remember one such little urchin knocking on our door and asking me:

"Are you Billy Franks?"
"Yeah, why?"
"You're fighting Paul Pearce in the football pitch at half past four."

I knew of Paul, and he was fearsome, so I tried to see if I could sneak out of it.

"But I don't even know the bloke," I lied.
"That's ok," replied the errand boy, "he's a fucking big bastard, you can't miss him."

I needed another tack. I lied again:

"Listen, I can't, I'm supposed to fight Johnny Kennedy at the monkey bars at five".
"Oh, don't worry about that, mate", said the little shit, "it'll be over long before then."

He was right and it was.

Jim was always a gentle soul and never wanted a fight with anyone. If he couldn't talk or run his way out of it, I would, now and again, be forced to fight for him. Strangely enough, I fought better and with more intent for him than I ever did when fighting my own battles.

As we all sprang into our mid-teens, there was also a sudden influx of families from Africa and The Caribbean. Fighting seemed to drop dramatically, and instead, music got a hold of us all. You could hear music coming from somewhere on the estate at almost any time of the day or night: reggae and ska from the blues parties on a Saturday evening, rock music from Fulham Court's own youth club, *The Blue Triangle*. You could lie in bed some nights and hear the entire Motown catalogue pleading with you to come join the party. There was always Beatles playing in our house. From the *Baxters*, you would hear Pink Floyd or ELP if Kenny had the turntable, or Chet Baker and Oscar Peterson if his dad, John, had it. For the *Hirons*, if Lee wasn't blasting The Eagles, his brother Mark would drown their block in the sound of The Who. Some Sundays, you could hear the echo of the same song from all corners of our block as everyone tuned in to hear the latest Top 40. After that, from the *Ellis* house, the old man, Big Jim, would have the crooners - Sinatra, Jim Reeves or Connie Francis - serenade us all over Sunday supper.

As none of our band members had jobs, we would rehearse in my bedroom during the week days while most of the residents were at work. You could hear the sound of stolen guitars and amplifiers from all over the estate, but never the sound of a complaint. Some of the mums would open their windows that backed onto ours, and shout requests across the courtyard.

"Billy Boy, play *Here Comes the Sun*" would shout Betty Ellis just about every day at around lunch-time.

The only person never too happy about it was Mum's boyfriend, Ken. He seemed to take it personally that while he was out working all day, an unemployed but fully fitted rock band was thrashing its way through

Beatles' songs in my bedroom. He and I fought over it constantly, once or twice even coming to blows. Ken always reminded me of that drawing you often see in old barbershop windows - jet black hair combed back and sprayed into place so that not even a hurricane could move it. He had a matching black goatee beard and moustache grown long enough to hide even the slightest hint of a smile, but he dressed smartly and had a fancy Rover car, so when my mother asked us kids if he could move in, we could quite easily see there just might be a few bob in it.

20 years earlier, when we were very young and still living in Battersea Bridge Buildings, my mum had, on a few occasions, brought home a very quietly spoken fellow with a heavily lined face under a flat cap which he never removed, even indoors. Apparently he had been tortured by the Japanese in a POW camp and had either burns or scars on his head. His name was Joe, and he was obviously very much in love with my mother. He would often bring sweets and toys for us when he came to visit. However, when Mum asked us all how we felt about him moving in with us, our answer was one that inflicted sadness on everyone concerned. *But what if dad comes back*? So Joe vanished from our lives and our mother continued to raise us alone.

By the time Ken had moved into Fulham Court with us, Karen, Jim, and I were already teenagers. He may have refurbished the place and paid off all the outstanding bills, but there was little chance his generosity would buy him some authority over three independent young adults who had learned the hard way to take care of themselves and each other. Only my little sister, Dawn, was susceptible to any step- fatherly discipline. She was tiny and pale. She seemed to hardly ever utter a word, but would simply observe the seemingly mad world around her through her perfectly round, pink rimmed, National Health Service spectacles. For Karen and I in particular, the weekly liturgy between Ken and us was, at least in hindsight, as unfair to him as it was funny to us.

Ken, I need money for school. Ken, I need money for clothes, Ken I need money for records. Ken, I need money for the weekend. Yet, should he utter the simplest of instructions, he would be shot down in a flash.

"Ok, kids, take your plates out."
"You're not my dad!"

To give my kid sister, Dawn, a little credit here, one time, Ken got an electric shock from a wall socket he was trying to repair that shot him half way across the front room. Dawn, who could only have been 10 or so, burst into hysterical laughter. It seemed to me like the first sound she had made in years. Her laughter sent Ken into a fit of rage and he sent her off to bed. A few minutes later, Karen and I were standing at Dawn's bedroom door to see if we could hear her crying. If we listened closely, we could just about hear Dawn singing, all to herself, in her squeaky little voice:

"Ken is a wanker, Ken is a wanker."

We hadn't been in Fulham Court long when a stage school down the road in Acton asked me if I wanted to join up. There was no way Mum could afford the fees, but they were willing to take me on for a year gratis.

A FAR CRY FROM SUNSET

Within a week, I bagged the part of Burgess in the film *Melody*, starring Jack Wild and Mark Lester; the big child stars of the day following their success in the hit musical film *Oliver!*

Melody was shot through the summer and I not only became friends with the two stars, but the girl who played the title role, Tracey Hyde, became my first true love.

Picture this: just weeks ago, I was a scruffy little urchin looking for any way out of the life I was bundled into. Now, here I was, fourth in the cast list of a major movie, playing football with two of the biggest young film stars of that decade and going through my first love with the movie's starlet. Even more surreal was the fact the film was itself about the tender yearnings of young love. In front of the camera, Tracey was in love with her co-star, Mark. When the set was broken down to reveal the real world again, it was my tiny waist around which she wrapped her arm.

After a day of filming in, strangely enough, my hometown of Fulham, the stills photographer took us four main cast members to Leicester Square to see *Oliver!*, which was still running in London's West End. I sat holding hands with Tracey for the whole two hours. At one point her thigh pushed itself against mine and I closed my eyes and just felt my whole body humming with young love. I was 12 years old and I had found the new world.

However, my acting was bad enough for a fair-sized role to be turned into a cameo in the cutting room.

When the film was done shooting, I would still go down to Surrey to see Tracey and her mum would drop us off at the cinema and pick us up when the film was over. I never invited them to my own home. Eventually her mum insisted on driving me home.

"I'd like to come meet your family, if you don't mind," she said.

So up to our second floor flat in Fulham Court we all three went. I felt like I was making my way to the gallows. I loved my family dearly, but what mayhem would greet us when we entered our home was beyond prediction. I knock on the door, our epileptic dog, Rex, starts howling and skidding along the hallway. Jim opens the door, topless and eating toast. My mum is chain-smoking through an episode of the popular soap opera, Coronation Street, and my sisters are sat on a couch that has straw sprouting from both arms.

"Would you like a cuppa," said my mum.
"No thank you," says Tracey's mum, "we really should be heading back."

I walked with my first love and her shell-shocked mother back to their car in silence. No kiss on the cheek, just a whispered goodbye followed by doors slamming, an engine starting and a car speeding towards civilization.

I never saw Tracey again and I joined the ever-swelling ranks of the broken-hearted.

I carried on acting for another two years but my heart wasn't in it. Then I was given the role of one of the lost boys in the touring version of Peter Pan. I was only 14, so had to use Jim's birth certificate to get a license. We toured the UK for three months, and it seemed that life on the road was where I belonged.

The opening night in Leeds, I went past the open dressing room door of one of the lead actors. He was sitting playing an acoustic guitar, his long hair hiding his face and half way down the back of his t-shirt that had a list of tour dates on it. He was singing Simon & Garfunkel's *Sound of Silence*. There was no train of thought. It was singular and explosive. I said to myself with such surety that it felt like someone else said it out loud, *"I'm going to do that, and I'll do it better than him."* I knew there and then who I wanted to be. I came home from the tour and bought myself a battered acoustic guitar. I practiced for hours every single day. I would walk around the estate and scrape my fingers against the walls to toughen the tip-skin more quickly. I had a copy of the only teach yourself guitar book I could find: *Play In A Day*, by Bert Weedon, but I soon tired of playing *My Bonnie Lies Over The Ocean* and *When The Saints Go Marching In*, so I bought myself a copy of The Beatles Complete Songbook and learned every song in it.

♦

It's show time at the festival. Mick is up at the production house to check which car of the convoy Elvis is in. Gary, Mike, and I are at the gate. Gary and I have cameras rolling. Mike is pacing nervously. It's a hard enough job to waylay famous artists like this, but when that artist is also your musical hero, it really gets the heart thumping. Add to that the fact that your conscience is always watching from the wings to see if the attempt turns into an honest approach or an ambush. Mick calls and tells us they're on their way.

In the distance, we can see a fleet of cars heading towards us, but Mick doesn't know what Elvis Costello looks like and as soon as they pass us by, the car Mick has singled out contains only two fat guys with beards and baseball caps. Neither looks remotely like Elvis Costello.

By the time we realize the mistake, Elvis's car is already behind the now shut gates. We've let him slip. Thinking quickly, Mike sticks his head through a gap in the fence and catches Elvis getting out of his Limo.

Gary, equally on the ball, is filming through another gap further along.

"Hey, Elvis! Can I get ya to sign something?" says Mike. To our relief, Costello turns, sees Mike's face squeezed into the gap in the fence and smiles.

"Sure," says Elvis and comes right over. As he's signing Mike's program Mike quickly runs through the premise of our quest: the tribute album, the unknown artist and the music charity.

Elvis has been around a bit. He knows, as we do, that if you don't keep your wits about you, you can easily be misunderstood and misrepresented.

"Great idea." he says but obviously wants the conversation to go no further and quickly jogs himself out of earshot. A guard then comes over and tells us we shouldn't be here anyway and to get the fuck out. It's a fair hit with some exciting footage. We're happy enough.

We had decided early into this saga that all we needed to do was talk to each artist and let them know we had chosen them. We wanted to make a fun road movie. We knew that organizing an actual tribute album was gonna take a lot of behind the scenes negotiation. A lawyer had actually warned us before we started out that even pestering these people to pose the question would get us into a load of trouble, and that we shouldn't even move until we had spoken to representatives of those artists on our list. That sounded like no fun at all. A little trouble was essential. Though, a little further down the line, the amount of trouble we would find ourselves in was more than even we were prepared for.

BILLY FRANKS

The Sacred Art of Leaving

(Scan QR code to download song)

4. Love Being Lost

We got out of New Orleans no more than a few days before Hurricane Katrina hit. It was a fleeting visit, but long enough for a brief love affair with the city. When I read of the devastation in the New York Post on a bench in Central Park a week or so later, my heart ached. We had no real business in The Big Easy. We were actually heading for Bay St. Louis, which is in the bordering state of Mississippi. Aaron Neville was playing a casino there, so we had our sights on another shot at him, but when you're that close to the home of Mardi Gras, you drop by and pay your respects. First, our regular tilt at the community cuisine. We've done this wherever we have travelled to. In Denver, we stooped low enough to nibble on some buffalo testicles. We each order one of the four most famous Big Easy recipes: Red Beans & Rice, Jambalaya, Gumbo, and Shrimp Creole, which, in accordance with our *own* tradition, we share among ourselves so everyone gets a taste of each dish. Afterwards, I persuaded the fellas to walk it off down on the banks of the Mississippi.

BILLY FRANKS

My most loved book of all time is *The Adventures of Huckleberry Finn*. My years as a boy by the river and my over-developed sense of adventure made Huck and me, brothers separated only by fiction. As Huck would sit by the Mississippi to think his way in or out of trouble, so I would take those steps down to the Thames to figure out my own predicaments. It was here I would sit under the stars and dream my dreams. I would hear music from the riverboats as they passed by. The River was going somewhere and the music was going too, and I wanted to make that journey along with them. When it got too dark or cold, I would sneak through the window back into our bedroom. I would often hear parties going on somewhere on the block. They had music, too, and I would lie through the night listening to crooners and rock and roll bands from far off rooms.

Whatever troubles I had, I felt music was my sanctuary. I knew it in a way no one else seemed to. I knew it by love. I understood it. I knew it as magic made by magicians, and I wanted to know it's secrets.

A friend of my mother's was throwing away a small transistor radio that had died. I begged her to let me have it.

"It's broken," she said.
"I'll fix it," I said.

In the one bedroom that all four of us kids shared, I took the radio to pieces. There were a few hanging wires. I tried connecting them together in every possible combination, each time feeling the little stab of disappointing silence. I touched them to the little lumps of silver on the transistor board. Nothing. Suddenly I touched two of the wires to the same silver spot and heard a tiny crackle of music. My heart skipped. I heated a knife over the gas stove and somehow welded the wires in place. It worked. Now, every night, while my brother and sisters slept just feet away, I would tuck the tiny transistor radio under my pillow and listen to Radio Luxemburg. I was reunited with my sweetheart. I imagined her drifting in from another side of the world; making her way along the river and up the steps where I sat and searched my soul, to slip in through our bedroom window and slide in next to me. Whatever troubles the day would bring, I had music to soothe them away before I slept at night.

♦

A quick drop off at a local New Orleans laundry, then a night on the town. New Orleans is one of those rare cities that is as brilliant and predictable as you pictured it: all neon light and blue music, with a parade of revelers merrying their way along Bourbon Street. We strolled from bar to bar until we're stumbling from bar to bar. We tried every shot the belted girls could fire at us until we eventually careened back to our hotel for some shut-eye.

I suffer from acute wanderlust, and a lot of my world-wandering has been done alone. When you travel alone, not only are you more inclined to draw strangers into your life, but you're also more likely to be drawn. I have friends in cities the world over that came into my life when both of us were between trains. (I used to buy myself a silver charm from every new city or town I visited. I wore them all on a chain around my neck until eventually they started to weigh me down. Now I travel with these three friends, and the charm of the road is even greater. It's golden.)

Four early morning hangovers in one car should have guaranteed us a quiet start to our trip across the border. But we're riffing on a hundred different gags before we are even out of Louisiana. We enjoy our own company so much sometimes that it renders us incompetent for a job as meticulous as this one.

We were a hundred miles out of New Orleans when someone asked the whereabouts of the CD with the song, *Love Being Lost*, on it, for Aaron Neville?

"It's with the flyers."
"And where are the flyers?"
"In Billy's guitar case."
"And where's Billy's guitar case?"
"Back in the hotel room in New Orleans!"

We travel thousands of miles to grab a fleeting moment with an artist, and we have nothing on board to distinguish us from what we know we sometimes can be: a quartet of big- talking drunks!

We pulled up by the casino which is actually a big old steamboat. The State law says no gambling within State borders. So some shark opened a casino just six feet from the shore. You think this would make it easier to infiltrate. Not at all; the place was a fortress. We had all but one of our cameras confiscated. We interviewed the usual informants; porters, maids, cleaning staff, etc. You never know when the slightest tip-off will turn into a trail.

We got nothing. I remembered I had a contact in Nashville who had claimed, when I met him on a trip to the island of Malta, that his law firm represented Aaron Neville. We found an empty hallway to the side of the casino floor, and I made the call. As I was waiting to be put through, a chubby, middle-aged guy with straggly grey hair walked past. Mick is, of course, filming my call in case it leads to something. The old guy is intrigued:

"That boy must be pretty important if you're filming all his calls!"

"Oh we're just waiting to find out if it's a boy or a girl," Mick joked. The old guy thought it both true and cute.

"Nah, I'm only kidding." said Mick, and he and the old guy started to talk. Now I don't know why in hell's name Mick asked the guy this next question but his very words were:

"You don't happen to be Aaron Neville's tour manager, do you?"

"Yeah," replied our new best friend. "He'll be here later on, you guys wanna meet him?"

I believe in a charmed life. If you go out into the world and do a little charming yourself, the nature of the world around you changes. It gives itself up to you in the sweetest of ways. There are probably only two or three people on the entire planet that you could put that question to and have them answer in the affirmative, and somehow Mick talked to him.

The guy introduced himself. "Adolf, pleased to meet you all." It's not a name you could ever expect anyone to introduce themselves as; he saw our reactions and told us the story.

"I grew up with that name, and one day I turned to my dad and said, - Dad, why did you have to go and call me Adolf? My old man says, - Son, we can't let one man ruin a perfectly good name for everybody!"

Well this Adolf is certainly doing his part towards the name's rehabilitation. He gives us tickets for the show, the keys to his room, and says he'll call when Aaron arrives.

We went to his room and lazed around for a while. The temptation to raid his drinks cabinet was intoxicating in itself. But when a guy is helping you out like that, you just don't do such a thing... do you?

♦

Before Scruff's first ever gig, we went by the local art centre to see if we could use the place for some rehearsals. It was run by a lovely old gay guy called Cecil. He not only let us rehearse there, but said we could settle in for the next two weeks, even stay overnight if we wanted, and all for free. Thanks to Zeppelin, Quo and of course 10cc, we had almost everything we needed apart from some decent P.A. speakers. I was keeping a journal at the time. I had won a competition in The Melody Maker and the prize was a collection of Linda McCartney's pictures with a diary combined. Here are some entries from that first week at the arts centre:

Tuesday: Cecil has been really kind, he let us have this great place to rehearse for free!

Wednesday: Cecil helped us put up a stage to rehearse on. He can't seem to do enough to help us out.

Thursday: I can't believe Cecil. He is doing everything he can to help get us started.

Friday: Stole Cecil's speakers!

♦

Up in Adolf's room, the excitement of it all is making us act like kids. All four of us are jumping up and down on Adolf's bed having a pillow fight when the phone rings. Mick answers; it's Adolf. He tells Mick that Aaron has just arrived and we should hurry down to the lobby to meet him. We don't want to swamp the guy, so Mick goes it alone while we stand back and film with the one camera security didn't find.

Mick catches him right by the lobby door and has a good long chat. He tells him all about the project, and how we're doing so far. Aaron is intrigued and says, "Yeah, get my details from Adolf and send me a copy of the song and some background stuff to look through and I'll see what I can do." Another hit. Thank you, Adolf. Forgive me, Cecil.

Love Being Lost

(Scan QR code to download song)

5. This Evil Man

I took the title of my song, *This Evil Man* straight from a tabloid headline. A man accused of a series of attacks on women had been caught, and those three words were above the picture of his blanket-covered figure being dragged through the gauntlet of a shrieking mob.

The word that stood out for me was not the obvious choice, *Evil*, but the last word, *Man*. He was a man. The usual tabloid moniker given to such wretches is "monster" or "animal". We prefer that because we don't want to imagine for one second that they are of the same species as the rest of us. How could someone get so far from the kinder heart that beats, albeit a little quieter, in even the worst among us? It hurts to consider. The child abusers we understandably revile today were most likely the victims who, few decades before, would have received nothing but our sympathy. It's a frightening trail of thought, but I got a song out of it.

Who among pop's current conservative elite would dare take on such a challenging piece? The artist we chose was much less well-known than the others but much more respected: Steve Earle. I think of Steve as a modern day Johnny Cash, a writer with courage. He's a good choice.

We were back in London as I had a gig at The Troubadour. That meant I could get Richard, my band's driver and tour manager, to drive us up to Steve Earle's gig at The Manchester Academy. Richard is someone you could trust with your life, but not with directions. We spent more time driving around Manchester looking for the venue than we did getting there from London. Myself, I don't drive. I don't even know how. While all my friends were taking driving lessons in stolen cars, I was teaching myself to play Beatles songs on my battered old acoustic guitar. Plus I daydream. If I drove, my mind would wander and so would the car, and someone could lose their life.

Twenty years earlier, someone's mind did wander and someone else could have lost their life, only I'm not the wandering mind behind the wheel and I am definitely not daydreaming. I am living through a full-blown nightmare.

A FAR CRY FROM SUNSET

♦

I am cycling down the Wandsworth Bridge Road. There's a crossroads at the foot of the bridge and, though I want to go over the river, I have a 30 foot, double wheelbase truck on my right. I check his indicator and he is obviously going over the bridge too, as he isn't signaling otherwise. The lights go green and I start pedaling hard to get up onto the bridge, but as we reach the crux of the crossroads, the cab of the truck, to my horror, starts to turn left. This thing is huge, and I have to reach right up to bang on the driver's door. This must be some kind of mistake. The world has got it all wrong. He hasn't heard my frantic banging, and the cab continues to plough into me. The next thing I know, I am underneath the truck, facing forward with wheels running either side of me, watching my bike get mangled by the front pair. I am screaming. He has to stop. I lift my head a little, and something hanging on the underside hits the back of my head, and I am spun out to the truck's right side. In absolute terror, I look to my left to see a double set of wheels about to roll over me.

I am crushed. The wheels miss my head by inches, but crush everything from my neck to my knees. The last thing I hear before I pass out is the sound of my own ribs cracking. After one turn of the wheels, I am stuck to them. On their second turn again I am dragged up inside the mud guard and my body is twisted. I am flying in and out of consciousness, screaming with the pain and the overwhelming terror. I come around briefly to find the truck still on me. To my left, I can see what turns out to be my hip and half my pelvis on the road next to me. My back, layers of skin peeled away, feels like it has a blow-torch fired at it. Blood is swelling all around me. I pass out again. I wake to find a man holding my face in his two hands.

"Don't look son, don't look." he says.

But I look and see firemen cutting away at my left side. I think they are amputating, and I start screaming at them.

"Not my leg, please, not my leg!"

The truck is still on my battered body; the driver is in too much shock to even move from his cab. Eventually, a police officer takes the wheel and gently reverses. In white, blinding pain, I pass out again. I wake up in the ambulance. I'm still a bloody mess and ranting at the paramedics to put me out, but I am so close to death that any anesthetic would take me over the line. I find out later that the ambulance crew had told the police officer to mark it down as a fatality. I wouldn't even make it to the end of the road.

I surface again, and I'm in the Accident and Emergency ward surrounded by doctors and nurses all frantically dealing with different parts of my body. Suddenly, my mum bursts in through the swing doors. She sees the state of me and breaks down.

"Get her out of here," I yell.

Once she's gone, a doctor, holding what looks like a hand drill, asks me what I'd eaten so far today. I scream at him too.

"What fucking difference does that make? Just knock me out, please, knock me out."

"Son," he tells me, "If you don't do exactly as I say, you'll be dead in two minutes. Your spleen has burst and you're about to drown in your own blood."

"Four Weetabix."

He drills a hole in my stomach to let the blood spill out before it fills my lungs.

I wake up again in pre-op. I can't believe I am still conscious and still on fire with the pain. I plead with the anesthetist to put me to sleep.

"Any minute now," he says, and tells me I have had 15 pints of blood poured through me to keep me alive. I hear just the last words of that sentence before I finally find the oblivion I have been begging for.

♦

Richard had finally found the place we'd been hunting for. We thought it might make for some nice footage to interview some fans who are waiting in line to get in. We ask them what they think our chances of getting certain artists to take part in a venture such as ours. The consensus seems to be that Rod Stewart would be the toughest and Steve Earle, the most likely. I am talking to this guy, Roger, who, only minutes before, had his picture taken with Steve Earle at the stage door. I gather the crew and, with cameras rolling and Gary armed with the microphone, we run around to the back of the building. We are there only a minute or two when Mick sees Steve Earle heading for the backstage doors.

"Hey, Steve", Gary calls out. "Can we talk to you for a minute?"

Steve Earle was very gracious and stopped to chat even at the sight of two cameras pointing his way.

♦

I wake up in the intensive care unit. I have a breathing apparatus stuck down my throat, tubes in both arms, my stomach and my chest. I have traction weights attached to a pin through my left leg, a splint on my left arm, and a morphine drip plugged into my right. I can barely move anything, but there is something I have to know. I slowly shuffle my right foot across the bed towards my left. It sends shooting pains through my middle bones and I have to keep stopping to let the pain subside. I finally get my right foot to graze my left leg. It is still there and, relieved, I fall back into nothingness. The next seven days are an opiate- induced blur. Friends and family come and go, but because of the tube down my throat, I can't talk. With my left arm in a splint, I am forced to scribble short notes right-handed. They are even less legible than the ones my old form teacher found so amusing. A guitarist friend, Tony, comes to sit at my bedside. Like so many visitors at this time, he finds it hard to find the right thing to say.

If you're a songwriter, it is considered that no matter what tragedy befalls you, how hard your heart is broken or how anguished your soul might be, you'll be fine: "You can write a song about that."

So here I am, pinned to a hospital bed, crushed to within a second of my life and my friend says:

"Hey, Billy, you could write a song about this."

I roll back my eyes and hope the morphine will deaden my frustration, but Tony isn't finished yet.

"I don't mean to be funny, mate," he says, "But I do know what you're going through."

I find it hard to believe anyone on earth could know that.

"Once," he continues, "I had this in-grown toenail…"

Scribbling notes was hard work, but I managed to scrawl a few words on a tiny piece of paper and hand it to my sister, Karen. "I think I need to be alone."

♦

At the stage door, Gary is equally struggling for the right thing to say. Gary hasn't had to interview an artist on the trip so far, so is understandably nervous. Steve Earle somehow retains his composure as Gary, fumbles and mumbles his way through the premise. Mick and I are in physical pain trying not to laugh as Gary tries to find his way through a verbal maze. By the time he gets to the big question, the camera I am holding is literally shaking where I can't control my laughter any longer. Steve Earle meanwhile has started to glaze over. He has now realized where the conversation was going, but he remains patient and kind enough to give us what has become the routine response. He tells us his manager's phone number and address and says to send the song and the film premise down to Nashville, and he'll take a look at it.

With Steve Earle safely inside the building, the three of us fell to the floor. I was laughing so hard, my jaw felt like it might break. Then, with cameras still rolling, Gary asked me to do an impression of him interviewing Steve Earle. I ditched accuracy for laughs and tried to nail the spirit of it.

"So Steve, you've heard of these things called songs, right?"

Gary is doubled up.

"Well apparently there are people who actually write them!"

Mick's gone now, too, and I can hardly speak through my own laughter.

"Now is that something you would consider doing?"

It's my favorite day of our travels so far: a full interview, on camera, with one of the artists, and an aching gut from uncontrollable laughter. We spent the evening painting the town of Manchester a very bright and blazing red before entrusting Richard to somehow get us back to London. Guided by satellite navigation, road signs, or even the star of Bethlehem, we knew it was a journey that could take either hours or days.

A FAR CRY FROM SUNSET

♦

I lie in ICU shifting in and out of a morphine haze. The breathing tube down my throat keeps my mouth agape and I feel in a constant state of gagging. I am kept alive this way for days. Having it pulled out is even more disgusting, but I cry with relief when I see the tail of it leave my lips. My lips are crusted and cracked. My sister, Karen, is sitting by my bed nursing a book in the crook of her arm like a baby. A halo of light gives her head of honey-colored curls an angelic glow. My voice is barely audible and feels like a faint breeze passing over gravel, but I need something for my burnt lips.

"Karen," I whisper, "can you pass the Nivea?"
"I love you, too." she replies.

I don't have the heart to tell her she had misheard me so I suffer a little longer before asking again.

My stay in hospital had lasted three months; hot-wired to the bed by tubes and monitors made every minute an eternity. I would try to not look at the clock, but desperate curiosity would get to me. It must be at least midday, I would tell myself, hours surely having passed since I last looked at 6am. 10:15, it taunted me. I could cry as I heard the tick of that clock chop my life into slow and painful slices. I never slept, which only added to the endless parade of minutes that took hours to pass. Late one evening I saw Clive The Vicar (in Fulham Court everybody was given the nickname according to their vocation; Clive The Vicar, Pat The Milkman, Bob The Taxi, even the local football coach who was always casting rather lustful looks at the younger boys was known as Vic the Bummer), walk past my ward. I found out months later that Clive the Vicar had been called in preparation of administering my last rites.

I am not a religious man, but had I been at all conscious while he was doing so, I may have had to confess that it was Lee and I who had removed the speakers from the Methodist church he ministered only a few years earlier. The organ, being fixed to the floor, was too heavy to move.

With my physical condition not improving, I decided I wanted out. I had fought through two more rounds of major surgery. I had shrunk to six and a half stone. I was kept alive by food tubes and drips. I had every kind of disgusting internal investigation at a doctor's disposal. I was cleaned, and cleaned up after by nurses of my own age. Enough now. No more.

The staff had taken to given me two sleeping pills at night to help me try and get some rest. But, as strong as they were, I would still lay there night after night taunted by the ticking of that cruel and relentless clock. My plan was to save the pills until I had around 25 (I had instigated a long but crafty conversation with a young nurse to determine the necessary amount). Then I would down the lot and be gone. But for all my afflictions, I suffer from optimism more than all others. I got to eight, told myself a good night's sleep would change my outlook, gulped them down, and got a few hours shut-eye.

A little sleep helped, but I woke to find myself still in purgatory. I lay in my bed with the curtains drawn around me for days. I wanted no visitors. Even when family and close friends showed up, I would have a member of staff take them away. I had grown disgusted with what I had become. If I wasn't going to take my own life, I wanted to at least spend it alone and in the dark. Late one night, I heard the old guy in the bed opposite me, George, whisper to his neighbor.

"I'm so worried about young Billy," he said. "We haven't seen him or heard a word in days."

George's leg was amputated that day and he had lain in bed sobbing after he came back from theatre. He hadn't yet even tried to walk with his new crutches. But he did that night. I heard him fidget and quietly moan as he struggled into them. Somehow, he managed to get across the room and through my curtains to sit on the side of my bed.

"I know it's tough, son," he whispered. "You've been through hell. But you've made it this far. Don't give up now. You're young; you got a whole life ahead of you. Hang on a little bit longer. You'll get better, you'll see."

And with that, he hobbled back to his bed. I sobbed at the thought of that old man putting himself out like that to comfort me.

A few days later, I had one final operation that seemed to straighten everything out, and I slowly started to recover. Soon, the traction and tubes were removed. Now the pins were pulled from my leg. I was able to stand on crutches for the first time in two months. I felt gigantic, towering. Nine weeks laying horizontally made standing up vertiginous. Now I would start hydrotherapy, a work out in water to provide slight resistance to my 7 stone wasted body. Since leaving intensive care I had only looked down at my penis two or three times and each time it was as black and lifeless as the last. I hadn't had even the slightest erection during my whole stay. It looked like a big clock's hour hand hanging lifelessly at six o'clock. I was wheeled to the hydrotherapy pool wearing hospital-hand-out, scratchy nylon speedos. The therapist and the porter lowered me into the shallow end, and various floats were attached to my arms, legs and neck. The early exercises were easy. Then I was literally put in a position that caused me to blush. The therapist who had large breasts bursting from her bikini top pulled each of my legs under her armpits and placed her hands firmly on my arse cheeks. Now my blue-nylon covered, flaccid-black penis was pointing at the first pair of tits I'd seen in almost three months. I went from atheist to agnostic and took a shot at silent prayer.

"Right," she said "I want you to sit up until we are almost face to face."

Fuck it. Dear Lord. Not now. I did three of these which gave enough gentle friction for my penis to shift to eight. When all else fails try a pact with the devil: "Please, not now!"

"Very good" she said, "keep it up."

She was in a league with Satan herself, how else could she be so cruel? Try to understand, I was gloriously happy the wedding tackle still worked, but we were now talking 10 o'clock and there was no way my skimpy penis-sheaf-as-swim-wear could hold back the midnight hour.

"Give me just a few more," she whispered.

I did two before the time I had been dreading came around. It was midnight and the head of my erect black cock poked its head out from under the feeble waistband. I saw it, she saw it, and her face looked as red and burning as my own face felt. She mumbled something but I didn't hear it. I just pulled myself free from her now loosened grip on my arse and sent myself floating towards the silver stairs. My blue nylon sail with its black masthead almost guiding me to that glittering stairway where I could make my escape.

A few days later, my sister, Karen, brought a guitar in for me to play. I was able to leave the bed and go to the television room to watch a film or two. George had been right: I was on my way back.

A few weeks later, George and I checked out at the same time. He on crutches, me in a wheelchair. It was a lot more sophisticated than the one Scruff used to tour with, but I didn't fancy it was strong enough to carry me *and* the gear.

It was almost two years before I could walk again unaided. During that time, I was often asked by friends what the extent of my injuries was. So, I'd tell them: a crushed sternum, entire rib cage shattered puncturing both lungs, pelvis broken in five places and twisted into an S shape, hip bone crushed and detached, spine bent, spleen burst, a severed bladder and one kidney squashed beyond repair. To which the response was always:

"Man, you were lucky!"

As funny as I always found it, it was the truth. I was in one piece, I could still sing, and I could still play that guitar. I couldn't wait to get back to doing both.

A FAR CRY FROM SUNSET

This Evil Man

(Scan QR code to download song)

BILLY FRANKS

6. Sing It One More Time for the Broken-Hearted

Before their demise, Scruff did manage one TV appearance on an afternoon kid's show called, *Get It Together*. We were billed in the TV Times as "the new teenage heartthrob sensation!" We had also made the pages of a handful of teen magazines. Lee and I both adorning the Page Three pin up section of *Oh Boy*! magazine; shirts open and thumbs in belt loops. But our one single for Track Records, *Get Out Of My Way*, hadn't done so well and we were dropped. I am not trying to slip the blame, but *Get Out of My Way* was the only song I ever sang that I hadn't written myself.

It was a song from our guitar player, Vince, who was a little older than us and had a head start in the songwriting stakes. My first-ever written song, though, did make the B-Side. I penned it only weeks before and was proud to see my first composition pressed into vinyl. That was until I was listening to Radio One late one evening. The

DJ was John Peel, a king in the country of the cult and the cool. If John Peel gave you the thumbs up, you got the keys to the city. Thumbs down, and you were bolted for ridicule in the village stocks. He was busy explaining how there were two kinds of songs he hated more than others. Those that started with the words Rock and Roll, *(Rock and Roll Heaven – The Righteous Brothers, Rock and Roll Band – Boston*, etc), and just as bad, to his mind, were songs that ended with the word Woman, (*Black Magic Woman – Santana, American Woman – The Guess Who, and so on)*. The name of my first song ever made immortal at 45rpm? – *Rock and Roll Woman*.

A few months later, we called time on our first band, and Lee and I decided to go it alone.

I had a song, *The Tradesman's Entrance* that I felt was something special; special enough for me to sell my beloved Telecaster guitar to pay for a day in the studio and the pressing of 250 singles. Instead of trying to sell them, we sent them to all quarters of the music press under the guise of it being an official, real-label release. We called our fictitious label FBI (Faith Brothers Incorporated). After a month went by and we'd heard nothing, our heads and hearts dropped and we took a week's holiday in Devon with family and friends. We came home and checked that week's music press just in case, but not a word about us was printed. Writing a song is the nearest I will ever get to giving birth. Two trains of thought conceive it: I let it gestate for a while before initiating its painful delivery into the world. I then nurture my offspring to be the best they can be before dressing them up well enough to go out and make their own way.

A FAR CRY FROM SUNSET

Sometimes it breaks my heart to find the rest of the world doesn't love them as much as I do.

A few days after our holiday, I was visiting the house of friends, Katie and Brad. Flicking through a copy of the popular, glossy but credible *Jamming!* magazine I saw, tucked in the bottom corner of the singles page, a review.

The Faith Brothers – The Tradesman's Entrance. (FBI)

This cruelly ignored single has been out for months now, but is simply too special for me not to write about. It is rare indeed to hear a political ballad these days, but though 'The Tradesman's Entrance' leans almost towards Barry Manilow, it wins through pure emotion. Relying on a beautiful soul voice and some magnificent piano playing, this tale of unemployment and recession hits as hard as any frantic guitar- dominated attack on the Establishment could ever hope for. In the right hands, this could have been as controversial a hit as 'Relax' – because it is that commercial – but although others may ignore this, expect to read more about The Faith Brothers in Jamming!

I was blinded. I shook my head, rubbed my eyes with the heels of my hands, and read it a second time. Somehow, don't ask me why, I knew this was it. There was now, it felt to me in my heightened state of excitement, a way for me to go. The dimly lit road that had stretched before me became a dazzling avenue of light for as far as the eye could see. I was going somewhere; I was going to be someone.

Kate and Brad found it hard to take in too. The magazine had been sitting in their house for a week, but neither of them had spotted the extolment of our song. I took off to tell Lee, and we both ran to the phone box outside of Fulham Court to call the folks at *Jamming!*. Lee and I had already been making music together for more than a decade. We had been the best of friends a lot longer. Both our families were close and tight; his brother, Mark would eventually join The Faith Brothers. Lee's two other younger brothers, Jamie and Tim would become our touring crew. If the coming years were going to be successful ones, they couldn't be shared with a better friend or in better company.

The people at *Jamming!* went crazy when I told them who it was. They had been searching for us for weeks; they had even sent a scout to Liverpool. It turns out we had mailed all 250 copies without any contact information. Incompetence is nothing new when it comes to promoting, and I often wish there was someone I trusted enough to hand the baton to. Yet, what should have been a disaster, now seemed a masterstroke. The missing band mystery had half the major companies in London wanting to talk to us, and *Jamming!* magazine wanting to write a follow-up article.

The music industry calls this kind of hullabaloo "a buzz". The buzz became more like a roar when Jeff 'Skunk' Baxter of The Doobie Brothers and Steely Dan, came to town. Jeff was in London looking for new bands to produce. At EMI they told him:

"We do have this one band, but you have to promise to keep it under your hat, we're hoping to sign them pretty soon. They're called The Faith Brothers."

Jeff took the tape and loved it. His next visit was to Chrysalis Records:

"We have a band we're interested in, but keep it to yourself. We don't want other companies muscling in," and promptly handed him another copy of the very same Faith Brothers tape.

Then at CBS:

"We are interested in signing this band…"
Jeff interrupted the guy.
"Don't tell me, The Faith Brothers?"
"No," says the A&R guy.

But he is soon on the phone frantically calling everyone in his rolodex to find out why he is out of the loop and doesn't have a copy of the now legendary tape. That is how the music industry works. Everybody wants what everybody else wants.

♦

The next artist on the *Tribute This!* roll call was Rod Stewart, one of the great British singers, and whose early records were always blasting out from some late night party in Fulham Court. Hearing rumors about the making of *Tribute This!*, DJ Tracie Young invited the crew to appear on her morning radio show in Essex. Rod had a mansion in the listening area. Who knows, he may be tuning in.

Our first difficulty was that Richard was once again driving us to the studio. After a misguided tour of the surrounding area, we eventually found the studio car park with a patient Tracie Young standing waiting for us. Instead of pulling up alongside her so we could exchange greetings, Richard drove right past her and crashed the van into the studio barrier. He just ran out of road.

Interview underway, I told Tracie the story behind the song of mine we had chosen for Rod to cover.

"When I was younger, I used to play in an old bar down in south London called *The Old Leather Bottle*. Every Saturday night when the gig was over, the landlord would lock the doors and I would get my acoustic guitar, and we would all sit around drinking and singing old classic songs I had learned in my youth. It would sometimes go on for hours. Every time I would say I was done and couldn't sing anymore, someone would always plead with me to play just one more, just one more song. I have fond memories of those days, and so had written the song to commemorate them. It's called *Sing It One More Time For The Broken-Hearted.*"

We soon found ourselves back in Manchester yet again. Rod had a gig at the huge SECC Arena. For an aerial view of the grounds, Mick had climbed up, armed with a video camera, onto a newsagent's roof directly opposite while Gary and I hung around the backstage area making security nervous. If Rod Stewart came by and the pair of us was camera- free, he might be more willing to talk, and Mick could shoot the conversation from the rooftop. Gary had a camera hidden in his bag running to capture sound. It was pelting with rain, and after more than three hours, we were soaked through and about to give up when a tour bus pulled in through the venue gates.

We watched the passengers - a stream of band members and road crew, disembark. Gary and I managed to slip in through the gates and grab a quick word with the bus driver. Rod, unsurprisingly, he told us, doesn't travel with the band, so wasn't on the bus. While all this was going on, someone had gotten suspicious of our movements and called the police. Suddenly, there were sirens and screeching brakes. Two cars and a van pulled up, and a handful of officers clambered out.

Mick was told to get down from the roof, and the rest of us to move on or risk arrest. It now looked hopeless anyway, so we headed back to our hotel.

Rod's next show was in his home town of Glasgow. He might be out and about and a little easier to find if he's on home turf. The following morning, we took an early flight to Glasgow. We speculated that a day spent talking to the locals just might throw up some leads. We got a cab directly from the airport to the arena where Rod was playing. It was still early, and there was always the chance we could find a way in during the sound-check. At the venue, security was again very tight; the main back stage doors had two police officers walking up and down outside them.

Mick decided it might be fun for me to interview them for the film. I explained our movie premise, and asked the police woman what she thought our chances were of getting the tribute album made.

"Two percent!" she reckoned.
"What about our chances of getting to Rod Stewart to actually pose the question?"
"Zero percent!" she said defiantly.

She obviously considered herself a lot better at her job than we were at ours. She had a point - a point proved conclusively when I left the officers and found Gary interviewing a Rod Stewart lookalike.

"So Rod, would you be willing to sing a song on this tribute album to an unknown songwriter to raise money for the Youth Music charity?"
"Guaranteed," says the unconvincing lookalike, unconvincingly.
"There you have it, folks," says Gary, turning to the camera.
"He's in. Rod Stewart; a man of the people!"

I have a great friend in Glasgow: the best-selling novelist, Christopher Brookmyre. In the murky world of black-comic crime thrillers, Chris is the bravest and shines the brightest light. He had also been one of those brave enough to invest five grand in the movie. He'd liked my songs from my Faith Brothers' days onwards and had even used quotes from my work in his books. We met up with him and his wife, Marisa, at a local bistro. Chris had a tip for us. Apparently when Rod Stewart is in Glasgow, he will sometimes pay a visit to an old drinking haunt; *The Wee Barrel* in Paisley. We made a note of that, settled the bill and left. Luck was still following us, and the cab driver taking us back to our hotel, Davey, had an even better tip. Rod was good friends with celebrity chef, Gordon Ramsay. Ramsay had a hotel/restaurant in Glasgow called The Devonshire Gardens. Rod had sometimes stayed there during fleeting visits.

Bags in rooms, we headed over to Ramsay's place. After casing the joint, front and back, Mick and I stepped inside to the bar while Gary watched the front entrance. Over a few drinks we found out from a member of staff that there had been some cloak and dagger stuff earlier that day, and maybe Rod had moved in. We hung around a bit until our waitress told us she had checked the register and the rooms, and was sure he wasn't there. Her tip was The Radisson in the centre of town.

We grabbed the other two and a cab and sped on over to The Radisson. We quickly made friends with some guests and staff in the Radisson bar, but could find out nothing regarding the elusive Mr. Stewart. Then Mick got a call from the waitress back at The Devonshire Gardens. She had been doing some investigating of her own, and had found out that whenever Rod comes to Glasgow, he avoids hotels and stays with relatives. News like that has a hugely exaggerated effect when you have been running on adrenalin all day, seemingly closing in on your target. A little crestfallen, we decided there was no sense in hanging around. The trail had narrowed to the point where we could get no further. We downed our drinks and started on our way out of there. We were only feet from the door when the very same tour bus we had seen in Manchester the day before pulled up outside the hotel and dropped off Rod's band members. Trail wide open again, we ordered another round of drinks.

After a brief visit to their rooms, the band hit the bar. We slowly charmed our way into their circle. Mick and Gary had burrowed themselves deep in conversation with one of their crew and were making faces at me to suggest they were on to something. They made their excuses to the guy, and came over to tell me what they had. It was the best news we had gotten in a long time. The guy they had been talking to was Conrad, bass player in Rod's band. He was from Philadelphia, the same home city as my three friends. Gary and Mick had told him our story and, like so many of the supporting characters in our ragged tale, he wanted to help out. His instructions were to "get to Barcelona for Rod's gig there the day after tomorrow. Go to The Palau Sant Jordi arena. I will leave at the box office for you, four tickets for the gig and four backstage passes for the after show party. Maybe you can talk to Rod there and then." Again, the heart of the movie's premise had found us someone who could get us right where we needed to be.

From the Radisson, we headed to a late night club to toast our success. The next morning at Glasgow airport, we got an almighty kick in the teeth. In the middle pages of the local paper was a picture of Rod Stewart sharing a pint with the landlady of *The Wee Barrel*. While we had been out celebrating our scheming with Conrad, Rod Stewart had spent his evening at the very place my friend Chris had suggested he might. The thought that we could have had some chill time in Rod's local pub, selling him our story, hurt us badly. Still, it wasn't over. We were heading to Barcelona.

A FAR CRY FROM SUNSET

♦

The frenzy to sign The Faith Brothers had gotten out of hand. Gifts for my young daughter, Alison were being sent to the house. My mum, the only one in the family who had a phone, was getting a dozen calls a day from record companies both sides of the Atlantic. One afternoon, she knocked on my door:

"Billy boy, I've just had a call from some bloke in New York, Rob Dickins? Anyway he says he runs WEA. He told me to tell you, (here she quickly checked the betting slip she had made notes on) that he had heard the advance offers were up to 30 grand but he was willing to double it. Something like that!"

And off home she went as if having just passed on a little local gossip. Lee and I had spoken about it, and agreed that the escalating price we were going for wasn't what was going to make us happy. But having almost the complete set of record companies clamoring for your signature gave us a great sense of freedom of choice. That, in turn, couldn't help but make any artist happy. But happiness and tragedy are lovers, never far from each other's side. In the heat of all these negotiations, a tragedy took place that would literally tear heart and soul in two.

My brother, Jim, had his heel clipped by a car as he cut in early on a zebra crossing right outside Fulham Court. His head had hit the windscreen and was bleeding heavily. An ambulance had arrived and given him a compress to hold over the wound. Fearful of internal bleeding, the paramedics were trying to persuade Jim to go with them to the hospital just to be on the safe side. Jim reluctantly agreed, but only on the condition that my mum wasn't to know, as she would only worry. Instead, they were to send someone to fetch me. I was helping out at a bar my sister Karen was running in Parsons Green. A phone call came in and it was for me. A nurse told me Jim was in Charing Cross Hospital with a head wound. I asked how bad he was, but she wouldn't say. Her voice told me it wasn't minor cuts and bruises. I jumped in a cab and asked the driver to get to the hospital the fastest he could. When I got there, Jim had slipped into a coma. I would never again have a chance to speak with my brother.

♦

With the guidance of our lawyer, John Kennedy, The Faith Brothers had now whittled our choices down to two labels: WEA or Siren Records (part of the Virgin Records stable). We were leaning towards Siren because they were promising greater artistic freedom.

With signing time fast approaching, a visit was paid to my flat in Fulham Court by the UK head of WEA, Simon Potts. I made some tea and asked what he was doing here. He told me that in his hand was a briefcase with 10 grand cash inside. If we went with his company, he would leave it here, tax free, no questions asked. I had a baby daughter and was on benefits at the time. 10 grand was a lot of dough. I let him grin cockily for a few minutes before I answered him. I told him that maybe a younger man would snatch his money and shake on his deal, but that I wasn't looking for a pay day. I was looking for a chance to make the records I had yearned to make for so many years. He left, stupefied. Not one to give up easily, he knocked on Lee's door only round the corner from mine.

"I can't believe it," he told Lee. "I just offered Billy 10 grand in cash under the table to come with us, and he said no!"

Lee, in what I consider an eternal testament to our friendship said:

"Well, if Billy said no, then the answer's no."

As shocked as the man was, it wouldn't be the last desperate move that WEA would make.

Jim had now been in a coma for ten weeks with no real signs of coming out of it. The internal bleeding had squashed a large portion of his brain, and the damage was extensive; all he could move was his left eye. I had read somewhere that hearing was the last sense to go with a loss of consciousness, so I would stay some nights and sit by his bedside and read quietly from my favorite book, *Huckleberry Finn*. When your brother is in the state Jim was, *hope* is the last thing to go.

Eventually, the doctor in charge of Jim's case called the family to a meeting in his office.

"The sad news is, Jim will never get any better than he is right now. We've tried everything, but he will remain in a vegetative state. I'm so sorry."

My mum, my two sisters and I wept. The doctor was patient and when we had composed ourselves enough, he said something directly to my mum that was as sad a thing as I had ever heard.

"We cannot do anything to improve Jim's condition. But, if you would agree, we could choose not to treat any infection he would likely get, and let him pass away."

No mother can surely make such a choice. Jim was her son and her first born. She was inconsolable. Minutes passed before she lifted her head, wiped her eyes, and turned to me. I knew what was coming and I felt my heart bow to the inevitable. She begged me to make the decision for her.

I had watched Jim closely for so many weeks, and was convinced he was suffering. One morning I had walked in the ward to find two nurses trying to administer physiotherapy, and Jim was making spastic, jerking movements with his arms that had terrified me. I knew deep down what I hoped a loved one would do for me if I were in Jim's place.

"Let him go," I said.

Jim passed away on October 25th 1984. His funeral was held exactly a week later on November 1st. Most of those who attended came back to our place for drinks and an exchange of Jim stories, more often funny than sad. Mid-evening, there was a knock at the door. I opened it and two young guys from WEA Records were standing on my doorstep.

"We're so sorry, we know this is a bad time, but WEA have sent us over because word is you are going to sign with Siren tomorrow and we wondered if it wasn't too late to change your mind."

My brother cremated and mourned only hours before, and these people came to my house to talk business. I was in a fury. I told them that their move was despicable, and to leave before anyone else found out and a lynching took place. On the Friday, November 2nd, at 10:30pm, The Faith Brothers signed with Siren Records.

♦

In Barcelona, worn out from the endless travelling, we spent the afternoon down by the sea. After all, tonight was taken care of; we had tickets and backstage passes. Rod was in the bag. It was beautiful and warm, and we had the whole day free from tearing around. It was nice to have some lazy hours to look back on our adventure so far. As always, the thing funniest to all of us was our immeasurable incompetence being continually rewarded with astonishing good fortune.

We found a friendly looking outdoor café, and again ordered a round of local delicacies to share among ourselves. Mick was relaying how he didn't watch reality TV because all that humiliation made him uncomfortable, yet here he was shooting this movie.

"I've pin-pointed my own problem with it," said Mike about the making of the film. "I just have a fear of authority. I'm in constant fear of getting yelled at."

"Shut up!" shouted Mick.

I love the Spanish practice of siesta. We were staying at a quaint family run hotel, and we snuck back there for a nap. Tonight, we were A-Listers. We were going to be on the same side of the fence as the people we had been badgering for so many weeks at so many gigs. We woke up and dressed in a manner befitting our newly acquired status as insiders. It was time to live it up a little and bag a prominent name for the tribute album. In the cab over, we were all fired up about getting backstage and talking with the man, but as soon as we arrived at the production office there was a problem. Rod's bassist, Conrad, had only gotten two tickets and backstage passes. So again, we had to make the choice of who gets and who goes. The rest of the gang knew that watching big names in front of big crowds just made me pine, so I was happy to drop out. Mike dropped out, too, but his reason was simply kindness. Or maybe he was afraid he'd get shouted at.

So while Mick and Gary lounged in the A- list seating area, watching Rod strut his stuff, Mike and I found the world's tiniest bar and sat and cracked jokes and talked deep. Mike's a moral touchstone. We don't always agree, but when Mike differs with me, I listen hard because I know the size of his heart.

Eventually, we reckon the gig must be almost done, and we head back to the Palau Sant Jordi arena. We need to communicate with the others while we watch the stage door in case Rod should make a quick exit, but there's not enough signal to send even a text message. We have no way to coordinate. It's not too big a worry, Mick and Gary are guests at the after-show party, and they'll talk to him then.

Rod has a reputation of being difficult, and with Gary's nerves shot after his encounter with Steve Earle, Mick has again volunteered to stand in the firing line. From where Gary and Mick are sitting stage-side and Mike and I are standing outside, both teams have a clear view, from opposite angles, of a black, shiny limousine. To our horror, when the final song ends, we all watch with bitter disappointment as Rod is ushered quickly from the side of the stage into the waiting car. Gary and Mick try to climb the barrier to get to where the car is, but are jumped by guards. Mike and I consider climbing the fence, but there are armed police officers just yards away, keeping a careful eye on our movements. Rod is obviously not going to any after-show party. In desperation, Mick and Gary are shouting at him from behind the barrier, and Mike and I are screaming from the back-stage gates. The car doors slam and in a flash, he's gone.

Gone also is any good reason to hang around any longer. Gone is our real chance to talk to Rod Stewart. But most of all, having tracked the man through three countries, gone is most of our budget.

Sing It One More Time for the Broken-Hearted

(Scan QR code to download song)

7. I Wanna Be Your Country

Don't tell anyone what you think. Don't tell a soul what you believe. Don't tell them what you know, what you heard or what you've read. In particular, don't tell them what you're planning to do. Tell them what you took a shot at, when and where you rolled the dice, who you met and what stories you were told. Tell them what you've done.

I have said these things to nobody more than to myself. It's so easy to become sour-talked into believing the world is a dark and dangerous place. Worse, if you're not kept from harm by a fear-inspired, self-imposed curfew. Stay where you are and keep your head down. There are people, groups, and gangs out there who will steal your heart or your money; tell lies to and about you, open you up and bleed you dry. It's a cruel, tough, dishonest world, and if you make a move you'll get taken.

This is a great deception. The worst kind of lie proclaimed by the nation's red-top town-criers, and spread by the bitter and disappointed. Make a move and find out for yourself. The world is a beautiful place full of honorable people with great stories to tell. The big-hearted outgun the small-minded on every corner of every town. I know. I've passed through a lot of them, and I learned where to look. When you get there and you find them, life has a deeply set benevolence you could so easily have given up on. I once told my two daughters, Alison and Billi, when they were very young, that there are people in this world who may try to drag you down. There are others who will do anything to give you a hand up. Try to spend your time in the company of the latter. Not just so it will lead you to a better life, but also that you might learn to be like them.

On the road making this film with these three magnificent friends branded that belief onto my very soul.

♦

Mike had business in the States to take care of while Mick, Gary and I had chased Rod Stewart through Manchester and Glasgow, but he flew into London to pick up the trail to Barcelona.

He bundled out at Heathrow Airport to be told the city had been shut down. There were explosions throughout the capital and the death toll was rising by the minute. It was July the 7th, 2005. Suicide bombers had detonated themselves into oblivion on three tube trains and one bus, taking 52 passengers with them. As with 9/11, you watched the compelling horror unfold as its true repulsive and spiteful carnage was diffused through the TV screen. You would have to be convinced God was on your side to be able to live with yourself before inflicting such a brutal kind of misery.

I can only imagine Mike spent his entire cab ride into town in a state of utter shock and disbelief. Reunited with us, Mike took some time to ring home and reassure family and friends that he and the rest of us were fine. We then headed out for breakfast at The Half Moon Café. The four us sat, ate and drank tea while talking through the tragic events of the day before checking our finances. The Rod Stewart trek had hit us hard with the Barcelona trip still to pay for. We were really low with four artists still to get to.

Tom Petty had been picked to sing *I Wanna Be Your Country* from my album, *Genius & Grace*. With a long haul out to Connecticut to catch Bon Jovi coming up, we decided we would ask one artist the cheapest way we could: on *MySpace*. I requested Tom Petty's friendship and attached our proposal. If he accepted, he surely couldn't turn us down. He would have to help us out; that's what friends are for.

With a few inexpensive clicks, we now calculated we might just have enough to work on the final three. And to think there was a time, back in my time in The Faith Brothers, when I probably saw enough money come and quickly go to have fronted the whole *Tribute This!* project myself. But to give credit to Lee and me, throughout the Faith Brothers' years, the record company would only pay the band and crew while we were out touring. During the weeks and months in between, Lee and I took care of them and footed the wage bill. It's where a lot of our advance money went. But these were family and friends, so that's what you did. When the Brothers finally split in 1987, two years after our formation, I was as poor as when we started.

♦

I have always said I didn't want to be in a band with acquaintances or hired hands; I wanted to be in a band with friends. With a small fortune in the bank and a record company willing to pay wages, we put together a five piece band. It was with guys we'd grown up with, had gigged in bars and clubs around our hometown with over many years. First on the list was Gus. His real name was actually Steve, but he had nabbed the nickname because he went at a drum kit with such gusto.

He was also the funniest guy we knew. When we started touring, we'd always head to the biggest of our hotel rooms and Gus would always send us off to bed with sore ribs and an aching jaw. The day we asked him to join, he quit his job. We now had a rhythm section to be reckoned with. I have always loved the sound made by the mix of an acoustic and electric guitar. Lee's older brother was a wild electric guitar player heavily influenced by Pete Townshend. Mark is Gus's flip side. He had a quiet intensity and was gracious in dropping his fierce desire to wring the life out of his Gibson Les Paul and see how much power he could wring out of an acoustic guitar. Henry we had only really known for a few years but Henry was impossible not to love, a gentleman. And I can say without exaggeration he was, as a piano player, inching towards greatness. Henry had moved to Fulham from New Zealand a few years earlier. The first time I saw him play, I knew he was one I wanted, so I mercilessly pursued him until he caved and joined an earlier band I had going. There could be no other choice to play piano for The Faith Brothers.

We found a trumpet player, only a kid really, Will Tipper, but he played with old soul. Will had worked with a saxophone player who he believed was as good as any. So we drafted in the eccentric, restless and big- curly-headed, Mark Waterman. Mark didn't simply play the sax, he tore notes out of it as if against their will. He made it roar in anger. Our first rehearsals were pure joy, we had a dream band. A magnificent seven.

In the spring of 1985, The Faith Brothers were rocketing out of nowhere. Our first single, *Country of the Blind* made single of the week in both *Melody Maker* and *NME*. Siren was expecting a big hit. With all the attention, we decided to put on a show at London's legendary Marquee Club. We had put together a seven piece band and had rehearsed ourselves fighting fit. We had just finished the sound-check and we were all heading off to grab a pre-gig dinner. On the walk, I said to Lee:

"This place holds 400 people. Our last gig had about 20 people at it. My only hope is we get around 200 so it doesn't look empty."

He thought that was likely but I could tell he was as worried as I was. Strolling back to the club after dinner, I witnessed something that remains among my most treasured memories from my days with The Brothers'. Outside The Marquee was a queue that went as far as the eye could see. In front of its doors stood a sign that read: *The Faith Brothers – Doors 7.30pm. – Sold Out!* It was just after six. As we walked down the line, people were calling our names and thrusting singles at us to sign. It felt as if we had arrived.

At 8pm, with still an hour to go until we played, there were still a couple of hundred people stuck outside. I took about 100 of them with me round to the back doors in packs of 10 or 12, and kept dropping the security guard small wads of cash to let them in. The place was now jammed beyond capacity, but there was still a small crowd outside desperate to see the show. I spoke to the club owner, and he was nice about it, but told me there was absolutely nothing he could do.

"There must be," I said.
"All I have now is the record company guest list," he said.
"How many names on it?"
"Forty."
"Give it to me."

He handed it over and I tore it into small pieces and threw them in the bin.

"Ok, let in another forty."

The show remains one of the greatest we ever did. I lost about eight pounds, but felt even lighter when I left the building.

That week, the single got play-listed by Radio One, the biggest nationwide station in the UK. This meant around eight plays a day. Enough to give you a good shot at making the Top 40. I remember driving to a gig with the whole band and crew, all of us friends that had grown up together. Out of the radio blasts *Country of the Blind*. You imagined moments like this all through the days you gave up to daydreaming, then, one by one, they make that leap into the real world. The thrill rushes through you. It reminds me of when I was just a boy, with a transistor radio tucked beneath my pillow. Only it's my voice that crackles through the speaker, my song the world is listening to. And I hope there's someone out there who falls in love with that sound as much as I did.

But there's music, then there is music business and in the music business it felt like all eyes were on us. DJs were predicting "international stardom". Bands we had loved only months before were now coming to our gigs. Some of them even taking notes.

While on the road we got word that the big-fight boxing promoter, Frank Warren wanted to manage The Faith Brothers. His offer included signing the deal in the ring of a world title fight. Crazy.

I once shared a cup of tea with the well-known publicist, Max Clifford. He told me there were two worlds too dangerous for even a hardened pro like himself to consider working in; boxing and music. If he had to take on a client that worked in one of them, it would be boxing. Boxing is a brutal game in and out of the ring, so his choice surprised me. Over the coming months, I saw how close he was to the truth. The music industry punches well above its weight, but when it catches you, you have to try hard to keep your wits about you and stay on your feet.

On the B-Side of our single was a song of mine, *Easter Parade* about my country's part in The Falklands War. In particular, the Government's decision that those soldiers maimed and disfigured in battle would not be invited to take part in the victory parade, lest their unsightly injuries ruin the national spectacle. It was an outrage. On that Friday, the posters for the single, *Country of the Blind*, went up all over London. They showed a picture of the Argentinean ship, *The Belgrano*, sinking, having been torpedoed by the British Royal Navy submarine, HMS Conqueror, with the loss of 323 lives. There were many credible statesmen and commentators who believed that, because the boat was outside of the British-declared Total Exclusion Zone of 200 nautical miles, the sinking was illegal. The attack occurred 14 hours after the President of Peru, Fernando Belaunde, had put forward a credible peace initiative in which he described the war over the Falkland Islands as "two bald men fighting over a comb".

The posters stayed up over that weekend. Our single was dropped by national radio on Monday morning. One or two DJs swearing to never play another Faith Brothers record again. We didn't care; we were tough enough to pick ourselves up. We had great guns and we always stuck to them.

We had a year of touring lined up. Firstly, a few weeks opening for Bob Geldof's band, The Boomtown Rats. Bob had just put together the Band-Aid single and was a national hero.

Before we hit the road, we had a little unfinished business to take care of. While our first band, Scruff was struggling to find a settled line-up, we had, for a few months, a big, kindly keyboard player by the name of Steve Zetter. We had a tough rule book for our first band and, a little cruelly, we made Steve leave his job as a surveyor so he could rehearse full-time. With no money to pay rent, his mum threw him out. He stayed with his girlfriend for a while, but she thought he was wasting his time and dumped him. In the end, it all got too much, and he quit. No sooner was he out the door then we took his keyboard down to a second-hand music shop, sold it, and split the money between the remaining members. We never really ever felt too good about it.

So, on the day we set out for the start of the Boomtown Rats tour as The Faith Brothers, we drove the truck round to his house. In the back was a top of the range, two-tier keyboard with bass peddles, built in drum machines, and even a cassette recorder. It was an expensive piece of kit, but our record company advance allowed us to pay for our contrition. We knocked on his door and told him we had come to make up for our teenage cruelty. Then, the band and crew carried the huge instrument up into his living room. Steve couldn't stop chuckling, but there was no doubt he did so to cover for the few small tears we pretended not to notice in the corners of his eyes.

As the supporting act, The Faith Brothers were mercenary. Every night, we fought to make the gig our own, and rarely left not having won over a few hundred new fans. Geldof never seemed too pleased about it, but we had waited a long time to tear it up like that before a big crowd. We ripped through our 40 minute sets each night as if death was waiting in the wings. Before the tour was finished, we made an appearance on what was the current cool rock TV show, *The Tube*. The band all gathered around a little black and white TV in our dressing room. It was our first real television appearance, and we were child- like in our excitement.

Our next tour was with The Alarm, and man, we hit the ground running. We were playing scorching sets, night after night to astonishing receptions. There was, though, one gig on that tour we had been dreading: Glasgow's Barrowlands. It was feared by bands throughout the UK for having the toughest crowd in the land, particularly for opening acts.

We took to the stage with the sound of 2,000 booing Scots. Welcome to Barrowlands. It got worse. As we fired our way through song after song, the audience took to showering us with spit. It was dripping from my guitar and I couldn't open one eye it was so sticky.

Half way through the set, I then had to sing *The Easter Parade* solo with just my acoustic guitar while the band stood side-stage. The heavens opened and I was soon drowning in phlegm. All I kept thinking was I don't care how much you jeer or how much you spit.

This is our gig and we're staying until we're done. By the end of the song, there was a ripple of luke-warm applause. Could sheer determination be turning the crowd around? We played our final three songs fast and furious and with added venom, with each getting a greater reception than the one before. We eventually left the stage to almighty cheering. In the wings, we were the seven deadly grins. Were they really calling out for more? They really were. We got welcomed back for two encores, apparently never heard of before at that infamous venue.

On that same tour, we had just finished a storming set at a club in Dublin one night, and were sweating it off in the dressing room when there was a polite rap on the door. Our tour manager took a peek outside and turned to tell us: "U2 are here and would like to come in and say hello."

Greetings and compliments were exchanged, and the band took their leave to catch the headline act. A few days later, I got a call from our agent to tell me that Bono had called him and asked if we would open for them at Milton Keynes Bowl that summer.

As a kid, tearing about the stage before an audience of that magnitude is at the heart of the dream. Only months earlier we were playing for six people at The Kings Head in Fulham High Street. A few weeks from now, it would be more than 60,000. We were thrilled.

By now, we had gotten ourselves a manager, the young man who wrote the review in *Jamming!*, Tony Fletcher. He had pulled us out of nowhere. He deserved to be dragged along in whatever direction we were heading.

The Milton Keynes Bowl gig was a great day out. We got our family and friends passes into the back stage enclosure while the band ate lunch with Billy Bragg, REM and The Ramones. There was a small sense of unreality about it. At some point during the afternoon, Bono came to talk with me. The first thing he said was how he thought my song *The Easter Parade* was a beautiful song. That was cool. It's a song I was proud of, and it was good to know that the big names were checking us out, but then he went into one of his famous Bonologues. Bono was young back then and very passionate. One who was sure of his mission. Man, he could talk! He raged for a fucking eternity! Mainly about all the saving that had to be done; people, lost souls, the world, etc.... I was of a similar mind myself, so enjoyed the first exchanges, but he just wouldn't stop. The Faith Brothers were to be first on stage, and it was all I wanted to think about, so I snatched my opportunity to escape. I saw Billy Bragg enter the caravan that he and The Faith Brothers were sharing, and told U2's main man that Bragg and I were thinking of singing a duet and that I had to go practice with him. It was a bare-faced lie, but my head hurt. Later someone, from our record company tried to get us together again.

"Let's get a picture of you with Bono and I bet we make the *NME* next week!"
"Fuck off," I hinted.

In my life, I have met more than my share of the famous. From musicians in no loftier a position than my own, to high ranking members of the British Royal Family. From well-known villains to my own musical heroes. But not a photograph exists with me in the company of any of them. I never ask. It's not an attempt to avoid sycophancy; it's just not my style. It's like this: I could find myself shooting pool with the Fulham Court urchins I grew up with, or discussing theology with the Dons of Oxford and all I'm interested in is having the best time I can with whoever I am with and wherever I happen to be. Trying to get any kind of record of the time steals its value from you, so I try to keep it equal and even, and it works.

Less than a month after the U2 gig, Bob Geldof announced the Live Aid concert. The roll call was outstanding. We had toured with Bob's band, The Boomtown Rats, and shared an agent with REM, U2, Queen and others, all of who would be on the bill. This gave me the toughest call as band leader I would have to make: Our agent thought he could swing us a slot on the Wembley stage as the token unknown act. With the entire planet watching, it was the kind of exposure beyond any band's wildest dreams. It didn't sit well with me.

I talked with Lee, and we turned it down. To appear on such a bill at that stage in our development could only be a career move. We were filling only small clubs at this point. No one was going to donate money to the cause because we were playing, and it felt far too cynical a move for me to be able to live with, so I asked the agent to drop it. Coming from where we did and having worked pretty hard to get this far, our minor longing for fame and fortune was far outweighed by the determination to enjoy our success with integrity.

Of course, many times since, I have imagined how different The Faith Brothers' future might have been had we gone for it, but I still believe to this day that it was the right thing to do.

Later that same year, when The Faith Brothers were still attracting a lot of attention, I got a phone call. It was Pete Townshend. He wanted to know if we would open for him for two consecutive nights at The Brixton Academy.

I was somewhat surprised at getting the personal touch, but was excited at the prospect and I accepted. The cutest thing about it was, for the last couple of years, I had been listening endlessly to his solo album, *All The Best Cowboys Have Chinese Eyes,* and telling everyone within earshot that one track, *The Sea Refuses No River*, was, at that moment, my favorite song on earth. Now I would get a chance to tell the composer himself.

A few weeks later, we spent the afternoon at The Brixton Academy, loading in our gear and contemplating what looked like might be a night to remember. We were standing by the sound board in the empty venue when I saw Pete come from a door behind the stage and walk towards us. Now would be a good time to tell him. He said hello to us all and then asked me,

"Are you Billy?"
"Yes," I said.
"That song of yours, *Storyteller*, is my favorite song right now, can't stop playing it."

I was staggered. There was no way I could tell him my regard for his song now. It would sound as if I were simply returning the compliment, so I had to let it pass.

The gigs were magnificent and remain among my most treasured of The Faith Brothers' shows. After one performance, Pete Townshend poked his head round our dressing room door and, laughing, said:

"You fucking bastards."

There was a party on the final night at The Hard Rock Café, and I got a chance to talk to Pete again. I told him "The Sea Refuses No River" was my favorite song at that time, but he still pulled a wry grin as if I were just being polite. It's a sweet memory.

♦

Meanwhile, Tom Petty had accepted my *Tribute This!* 'friendship' request on *MySpace*. He never mentioned appearing on our tribute album, though. Some friend he turned out to be.

I Wanna Be Your Country

(Scan QR code to download song)

8. Sleep A Little Easy When It Rains

By the time The *Tribute This!* crew found ourselves in Norwich, Connecticut looking for Bon Jovi, we were destitute. We were sleeping four to a room at a rundown motel, and eating on the run. Walking to the motel to check in, I had said, laughingly:

"As we're getting to the end of our budget, the quality of our hotels is dropping dramatically. 200 bucks left in the budget? Look at this place! And remember all those great meals we used to get? I just had a hoagie in the back of the truck."

Gary replied: "Remember when we stayed at the Roosevelt Hotel on Sunset Boulevard in Hollywood? Now it's the Economy Inn!"

"Yeah," I said. "It's a far cry from sunset."

Bon Jovi was playing at The Mohegan Sun Casino. After a fitful sleep in the snoring emporium, we headed over.

With nothing safe to eat at the Economy Inn, Mick wanted to grab breakfast.

"Mick, are we looking for Bon Jovi, or eating breakfast?" I said.
"Both," said Mick, "we're looking for him eating breakfast."

We asked the cafe cashiers if they knew where Jon Bon Jovi might be.

"I don't know where he would be," said one of the girls.
"Could you charge our breakfast to his room?" I thought with our current state of affairs, it was worth a shot.

The song chosen for Bon Jovi was *Sleep A Little Easy When It Rains*. I had written the song after watching a biopic about the legendary American comic, W.C. Fields, who I loved. Apparently, he could only sleep if it was raining outside. Edgar Allan Poe is quoted as calling sleep "little slices of death". Well, on the night W.C Fields died, it poured.

The song had also once given me an opportunity to make myself a fortune.

A Nashville publisher had come into possession of a copy, and got in touch to tell me that he had a major, multi- million dollar selling country star who would remain nameless, but wanted to record a version of the song. There was one catch. The opening verse goes like this:

A FAR CRY FROM SUNSET

Demons assail me
Bad memories trail me
Drink and drugs fail me once again

The artist in question didn't want to spoil his wholesome image with the words *drink* and *drugs*, regardless of the fact that the song bemoans their failure. But here's the slippery part, in exchange for taking the line out, I would have to agree that the artist in question had co-written the song with me. It's a filthy trick, but not uncommon among major stars. Find a great song by a struggling songwriter and offer them the reward of a financial windfall for making the artist look more talented than they really, and rarely, are. It's despicable, and I was having nothing to do with it. I told the publisher it was my song and staying that way. I never heard from them again.

I have no religion. I have no God to worship or fear, and no heaven or hell to look forward to, but I do believe in the soul, though not a soul that will survive me, or that can be saved for an afterlife, or abandoned to eternal damnation. My soul was saved by music. My soul was nurtured and made deep and wide by music. If I were to ever sell my music for fame, money, or any other transient reward, I would be selling my soul. I would be a dead man walking.

◆

Relations between The Faith Brothers and the record company were getting strained. Looking back, I can see how and why.

The Belgrano poster for our debut single had alienated radio. The second single, *A Stranger On Home Ground* was a cracking song, but we had used the advertising campaign to nationally publicize the proposed flattening of Fulham Court. For us, bringing down our home estate was like demolishing an A-listed building. To the label's dismay, the album, *Eventide*, had made the lower reaches of the top 40 and went no higher. Worst of all, the label had persuaded us to allow the current pop-video wunderkind, Tim Pope, to shoot the video for *A Stranger On Home Ground*, overriding a pretty decent script I had penned for it myself. Tim's idea was for each band member to be placed in different room in an abandoned farmhouse. Meanwhile, I and a few equally confused farm animals would wander aimlessly from room to room as the band played. In one room, Henry, the keyboard player, had a donkey tied to his piano. The resulting video was an embarrassment. All these years later I still find it excruciating to watch.

The third single, *Whistling In The Dark,* got off to a bad start with Siren's refusal to fund another video. Relations were almost at full stretch and tightening a little more every day.

While the band was out touring with R.E.M, the label's head of A&R had paid a friend of his to remix *Whistling In The Dark* in preparation for its release. Back in London for a show, Lee and I stormed into his office and informed him not only was the remix to never see the light of day, but the recording costs, which are always added to the band's bill, would be stricken from our debt. He looked ashen when we left.

A FAR CRY FROM SUNSET

Our fourth single of that first year, the album's title track, *Eventide (A Hymn for Change)* was to be released at Christmas. Siren again refused a video budget, so we took the matter into our own hands in a way that proved that old habits do die hard. Lee and I paid a social visit to the label. With all the staff busy in their offices, we broke into the store room and stole the album's master tapes. These would be needed if we were going to shoot our own self-financed video. We had befriended a film-maker called Steve Graham through our sound engineer. He had a similar mindset to our own, and we hired him to shoot the four- minute film in an abandoned church in London's East End. It looked pretty cool. I sat and sang at the altar, while Henry sat at the big, beautiful church organ. Once edited, we touted it to all the major TV stations independently, and managed a few prime-time airings. Richard Branson, the Virgin head, lost his mind, and members of the Siren staff were fired. From now on, it was going to be a tough deal to get anything done.

But we had an unbeatable hand. Back when all the labels in the land were courting us, we had been able to have an amendment added to our contract that is rarely conceded by record labels. It is called 'Two Albums Firm.' It meant that Siren didn't have the usual option of dropping the band at the end of each year if things weren't working out. They had no choice but to fund and release a second record. Some kind of peace-making would have to take place.

During all this warring, another loss hit us all hard. Lee's father Dave died. Dave was one of those guys who had the knack of being a friend as much as he was your mate's dad. He was, in fact, Scruff's manager for a while.

He was funny and sharp. When we were growing up, I would often talk with Dave on topics of which I felt ignorant or ill-informed.

On the morning of his funeral, my girlfriend, Sue and I went to Lee's house to join the drive to the cemetery. It pained me to see Lee's mum, Bet, grieving so hard. She is a kind and beautiful woman, and she had, without question, lost the love of her life. I hugged her and she asked me if I would I sing something at the service. I was quite a mess myself, so I promised only that I would take the guitar in the hope I felt up to it when called. The thing I dislike most about church ceremonies, weddings, christenings and most of all, funerals, are how little the priest will talk about those we have come to bless or to mourn. It's always the relentlessly repeated tales from the bible concerning the adventures of Jesus and the gang. So when the priest finally asked if I would sing, it felt the best way to reclaim the service for ourselves.

We chose *The Faith Brothers'* song, *Eventide (A Hymn for Change)* because it was Bet's favorite. Henry, our keyboard player, sat at the church organ, and I sat at the altar with my guitar. The likeness to the song's video made it even more heartrending. I cried more than I sang, but I could feel the congregation had at last a chance to properly grieve. When they joined in with me on the chorus, I simply broke down.

Somehow, we made it to the end. I felt having Dave's loved ones sing a song of our own making was a fitting tribute and farewell to my best friend's father, Bet's lifelong sweetheart, and my own dear friend.

A FAR CRY FROM SUNSET

♦

One thing Mick, Mike, Gary and I have learned through the ordeal of trying to talk highly guarded rock stars into making our tribute album is to ask anyone, anything. You never know who might have that seed of information that could blossom into a new trail.

But if anyone at The Mohegan Sun Casino knows anything, they're not yet letting on. Scouring the casino floor for clues, we see a cartoon style map on a wall and take a look.

"Take a picture of that map on your phone," Mick tells Gary. "We might be able to use it."

The map shows the arena itself to be in a different part of the grounds, so we hop into the car and set off in the direction the cartoon map tells us. After circling the arena, we see a sign that reads: Authorized Personnel Only. Just what we were looking for. We drive past the barrier; a guard shouts, but we wave in a friendly manner, and he dumbly smiles back at us as if he was expecting us all along. We head underground until we're in the bowels of the venue. Parked all around us are huge trucks from which road crew are unloading band gear. This is the spot. We park in a darkened corner and keep our heads low.

We wait around for half an hour, but nothing seems to be going on. We decide that if the guard was stupid enough to let us drive through once, he'll be so again. So we drive out and go in search of other avenues. We head for the roof of the parking lot for a bird's eye view of the area. When we get there, Mick asks Gary a question.

"Gary, you got that picture of that map on your phone? Let's take a look at that."

I start to ponder our latest bout of ineptitude, and for some reason, I get the giggles. Soon it becomes full blown laughter, and I can't stop. The others look at me quizzically, but with grins on faces. I want to try to explain, but I've developed a fit of hysterics. I don't want them to think I'm laughing at them, so I try to smuggle an explanation through the laughter.

"Of all the plots we have hatched to get to a pop star, this has to be the worst!"

Fortunately the pathos of it has hit them, and they are laughing, too.

"Take a picture of a cartoon map, drive to the top of a parking lot where no one can see us, take a look at the map, then its 'quick let's get out of here!' That's how we decide to get to Bon Jovi."

Our desperation seems to have risen at the same rate that our finances has dropped. I know all of us are now remembering the lofty start we had made, and wondering how on earth it had now come to this. We laughed for so long, until, with comical mock pride, we took turns proclaiming our achievements thus far:

"We did show Huey Lewis our umbrellas!"
"And Tom Petty *is* our MySpace friend!"

"We did shout at Elvis Costello through a fence!"
"Yeah, we even jumped up and down on Aaron Neville's tour manager's bed!"

I swear we laughed until we cried. It was beautiful.

♦

With The Faith Brothers' second album, *A Human Sound*, on the shelves and a single, *That's Just The Way That It Is With Me* making a less than modest entry into the chart, The Faith Brothers took up an invitation to join Julian Cope on his UK tour. We had always got on fine with the headlining acts. Members of The Alarm are still friends today. REM were always cool and would often watch our sets. Many years later, their guitarist, Peter Buck, would ask his interviewer in *Q* Magazine,

"Whatever happened to The Faith Brothers, man? What a great band they were."

But Cope and The Brothers did not get along.

Our reputation as a 'live' act had grown to such an extent that major acts would refuse to accommodate us. Two in particular; The Fine Young Cannibals and Simple Minds were given the choice of us as their opening act. After checking us out at another show at London's Marquee club, both bands turned us down and both parties gave the same reason: There's no way we're going on after them.

Here's a quote from *The Melody Maker*:

"For all intents and purposes, they are the best white soul pop outfit since The Spencer Davis Group. The fever of the sextet, (two horns, guitar, drums, bass, and keyboards) is inspiring, thrilling. Not since The Jam hit CBGB's in 1977 have I seen a young group expend such unfeigned energy. The passion and – yes-faith are shiningly genuine."

From *Sounds*:

"The Marquee is sold out and enraptured. The Faith Brothers are loved and are going to be very popular. Making a big, blue-eyed, soul-derived noise, rarely letting up in pace. When they're wearing their optimistic, irresistibly ebullient overcoat, they are committed, unswerving, articulate, and fun."

On the Julian Cope tour, we were, of course, as mercenary as always, and winning hearts nightly. In the three weeks we travelled with him, he never exchanged a word with us, telling some of our followers:

"They're noisy and brash like a fucking football team."

Julian Cope saying what Julian Cope thinks Julian Cope should say.

The last night of the tour was at Glasgow's Barrowlands, the setting of an earlier hard-won victory. This time, we were received warmly, but before we left the venue, the soul of the big kid in all of us came to the fore. We got our road crew to break into Cope's tour bus and put itching powder in all the beds before we made our own cozy, long drive back to London.

A FAR CRY FROM SUNSET

♦

Down from the rooftop of the Mohegan Sun Casino in Connecticut, we were putting together the only bad-enough plan we could still afford.

We had managed to find out from a groundsman where and when Jon Bon Jovi's limousine would drive by. From a local stationer's, we bought three big colored placards and emblazoned each with simple instructions.

Gary, Mike and I would hold them in a row as the big black car drove right by us. Mick would be behind the camera on the other side of the pathway.

"Hey Jon Bon Jovi! We're Making A Tribute Album For Charity"
"To An Unknown But Deserving Songwriter"
"Honk If You Agree!"

Our informant was bang on. JBJ's limo took the small road into the Casino, and was slow enough and close enough for us to have whispered it to him, let alone for the singer to read our demands.

They didn't stop.

To underline our senses of both fun and desperation, I turned my placard round to show the retreating car what we had written on the flip side.

"Ignore Us If You Agree!"

On those terms, at least, it seems Bon Jovi was with us.

♦

Siren Records and The Faith Brothers arranged a sit down. Pretty soon, we had to get going on the second album. It was never going to work if we spent the whole time at war.

So, after a long and heated debate, it was agreed. We could record our next record without interference at a studio of our choosing. They would back whatever was chosen for the first single with a video budget using the same director we had used for our guerrilla shoot a few months earlier. The studio we chose? The only one that would fulfill another long harbored dream for all of us: Abbey Road.

We moved in and set the band up in the famous Studio Two. We lined ourselves and our equipment up as if for a gig. We were going to record these songs 'live'. In just three weeks, we had put down 10 of the finest songs of our career. Not only were the sessions vibrant, productive, and fun-filled, there was the added treat of often getting visits from various dignitaries wanting to see the very room The Beatles had recorded almost their entire catalogue of songs, including a strange and wordless afternoon spent in the company of the Princess of Thailand.

I will drop any pretentions of immodesty and just say it straight. To my mind, the album we made, *A Human Sound,* remains among the greatest undiscovered pop collections of that or any other decade.

A FAR CRY FROM SUNSET

To add to the joy of creating it, the record company set up an all expenses trip to Los Angeles to mix the songs. We stayed in poolside rooms at The Hollywood Roosevelt; the very same one the *Tribute This!* crew would spend a few nights at 20 years later, and that Gary and I would pine for as we checked in gloomily at The Economy Inn.

The Faith Brothers' stay in L.A. were great times. Greg Edward, who had produced REM and was co-producing our album along with Lee and me, would get to the studio early and set up a mix for that day's chosen song. We would drive over early afternoon, suggest any changes we thought were needed, then spend most of our evenings running up massive bar bills in The Hollywood Roosevelt Hotel.

When we checked out three weeks later, our bar tab was 12 grand. Siren called to inform us that our drinks bill had exceeded the cost of making the album.

♦

The security at the Mohegan Sun Casino had been monitoring our movements. Driving through the grounds, we were suddenly surrounded by flashing vehicles. One car was definitely not in-house security, and the two guys that got out of it looked high ranking and mean. One of them was way over six feet tall and almost as wide. He had his red hair greased back and his moustache neatly trimmed, and was also the best dressed of the bunch. As he walked toward our car, there was no mistaking he meant business.

We were given the full dressing down. We tried to argue, but he was tough and uncompromising. Whenever one of us would try to explain, he threatened arrest if we said another word. All through the scolding, we had been filming nervously and surreptitiously from the back seat. He caught us. The guy grabbed the camera and removed the film.

Luckily, it was a new tape and only had the footage of our confrontation. Next to me was the camera with all the earlier Bon Jovi footage. I could see him eyeing it up. If that went, we would lose everything shot so far that day. Mick was whispering to me while Mike kept them talking.

"Switch the tapes, man, switch the tapes!"

He dropped his hand behind the driver's seat and slipped me a blank. While Mike and Mick were trying to explain our actions as slowly and politely as they could, I managed to remove the tape from the camera and throw in the blank before the security chief told me, "I'll take that one too, young man." I argued timidly, so as not to arouse suspicion, and reluctantly slipped the blank tape out of the camera and handed it over. They then not only gave us a police escort off casino grounds, but through most of Norwich, to the welcoming sign of our beloved accommodation: The Economy Inn.

Sleep A Little Easy When It Rains

(Scan QR code to download song)

BILLY FRANKS

9. Alone With What You Know

We were busted. Flat broke. The money we had raised from sponsors had long gone. I had personally thrown in a bank loan and a two grand credit card and I, of the four of us, was a long way from being the one who had invested most. So desperate were we towards the end that we had asked my modest, but loyal group of fans, to make small online contributions to help keep us on the move. Their generosity never fails to move me.

I once put on a show at London's Shepherds Bush Empire and was talking with the guy who runs the venue in the bar afterwards. He told me that not only was it one of the better shows they'd had in the last two years, but that it was the sweetest crowd he'd had in the place since he took over many years before. He told me how he couldn't believe how much love and goodwill there was in the room. I have said it before: I may not have the biggest following, but they have been kind and loyal for so long that it would have been a much tougher struggle without them. I always feel the word 'fans' doesn't do them justice. I once sold out Ronnie Scott's in London and worked out that I knew the Christian names of almost all 340 people in the room. That night, something happened that captured perfectly the relationship we have.

Chris was from Cheyenne in Wyoming. He had been stationed by the American Army in Italy. Chris was a big Faith Brothers fan, and realizing Italy might be the nearest he would be to London in a long time, he flew over to watch us play at The Lost Theatre in Fulham. We were there for the afternoon to sound-check and, while making myself some tea, I saw a young guy hanging outside in torrential rain. I opened the back doors and told him to come inside to shelter and catch us running through a few songs, he seemed genuinely thrilled and started taking photographs. With this being a local gig, my daughter Alison, then only six years old, was also spending the afternoon with us. Chris kindly took a picture of the two of us sitting on the stage.

Forward 21 years. I am playing Ronnie Scott's club in London. Before we take the stage, a guy comes up to me with a gift.

"You don't remember me, do you?" he asked.

He seemed vaguely familiar but I couldn't place him.

"My name is Chris," he said, "and back in '86, you pulled me in from the pouring rain to watch a sound check at The Lost Theatre. I am here from Wyoming for the weekend to see you play tonight."

A FAR CRY FROM SUNSET

I really was taken aback. It was a long way to come to catch a show and say thank you for a small favor. His gift was a framed picture of me and my little girl from all those years ago. I still have it hanging in my hallway.

With the pot totally empty, I came back to London, and Mick, Mike, and Gary went home to Philadelphia. We still had two acts to propose the tribute album to. We were, somehow, going to have to work out how.

There was a call I had, at least to this point, kept myself from making. I had a long-time friend, Lucy. While working for a concert promoter, she had been really helpful to the rock singer, Bryan Adams, while he was moving into his London home across the road from her office. She had, in fact, introduced him to me once, and had given him a tape of mine which he had liked. Bryan Adams was one of our chosen 10. Mick had chosen for him one of his own favorite songs of mine, *Alone with What You Know*, an up-tempo rock song with a gospel-type chorus. I have to say, I imagined him doing a decent job on it.

I hate to call on that kind of favor from a friend, but we were up against it, and Lucy had a heart sweet enough that it couldn't hurt to ask. A flurry of emails were exchanged; Bryan and I never writing directly to each other. His main concern was this: the premise of the movie was such that we had the one question to ask him, on film, that we couldn't reveal until cameras were rolling; would he appear on a tribute album to an unknown songwriter? I promised it was a soft question and in no way offensive.

After a couple of days of digital conversation, Lucy called me. He had agreed, not only to be interviewed without knowing in any detail what we would ask of him, but that we could visit him at his London home only hours before his gig at the Earls Court Arena. This is a good as it gets. For the first time, we actually had some real face-to-face time with one of the artists we had chosen. To add to our optimism, Bryan had not so long before taken on a similar quest himself. He had asked a lineup of supermodels to pose for a book of photographs he was planning, with all the proceeds going to charity. He would understand what we were putting ourselves through.

So my friends dipped into their own pockets again, and flew into London. No such expense for me, Bryan lived only a few streets away.

♦

When The Faith Brothers' second album, *A Human Sound*, didn't achieve the success that we expected and thought it deserved, Siren Records' MD, David Betteridge, called Lee and me to a meeting. The label's two other acts - The Cutting Crew and T'Pau - had both had massive hits on both sides of the Atlantic, yet we had cost the label twice the budget of both of them. It was mutually agreed that it was a good time to part company, as The Faith Brothers owed Siren Records just under half a million pounds. If we split, the debt was written off. From the MD's point of view, we had been stubborn and demanding from the very beginning. If he wanted to wash his hands of us now that he was free to, you could hardly blame him. To give full credit to Betteridge, he did add that it was a long time since he had worked with a band with such sustained integrity.

For two years, we had been at the ball, but it was a dance at which the hosts dictated how you dressed, which music was played, and who you danced with. Rules no honest artist could follow. We were being politely asked to leave. For us, at least, the party was over.

For myself, my writing was going places I simply couldn't take company. Places I would have to go alone. The band of Brothers went their separate ways.

♦

About a month before The Faith Brothers had set about recording *A Human Sound*, I had locked myself for seven straight days into the small studio we had built in Fulham Court and recorded a mini album that had taken me the previous six months to write: *Saint of Contradiction.*

The writing of it had become a full-blown obsession. I wrote from the early hours of the morning till late at night, sometimes stopping only for hurried meals. It was a writer's search for faith. I wanted conviction. I wrote in a desperate hunt for something I could openly and honestly feel devoted to. The way I thought to find it was to crush, tear apart, and tear down everything I had been asked, tempted or forced to have faith in until now. Political, philosophical or religious, I didn't care.

I would demolish everything that I had ever been persuaded to believe in, that gives life meaning, even God if I had to. Using words with music, I sought to burn down every place of worship, shred every sacred text, and unmask every so called messiah. When I was done, if there was anything left standing, I would have something I could give myself up to. The writing of the piece took my mind to a place so barren that I had literally feared for my sanity. Those six months pushed me to the very edge of my mind's own abyss. When I was done, there was nothing left standing. For a period, I felt nothing but absolute loneliness. I had destroyed everything. When I looked back from the edge, there lay the ruins of all that I had never truly trusted. It looked like I was in Hell but I was in love. With everything else torn and stripped out of its way, love stood still and strong. Bright, patient and absolutely indestructible. All that had hidden love from view or taken credit for its power was gone.

A little while later, Lee's sister, Joanne, gave me a framed illustration by artist John Bauer, with the caption *'The Boy Who Was Afraid Of Nothing'*. She said she had bought it because it made her think of me. After the fearful time I had put myself through for the last six months, it was immaculate timing. It is still the first picture I hang whenever I move to a new home.

♦

I met Mick, Gary and Mike at London's Heathrow airport, and we headed back to my house to prepare for our meeting with Bryan Adams. We hadn't been gifted a chance this good, and we didn't want to mess it up. It was decided that, as the introduction was made through a friend of mine, I should put the questions to Bryan. I had met him briefly before, and he seemed a nice enough fella. No problem.

A FAR CRY FROM SUNSET

We took a cab over to his house and stood outside for five minutes to collect our thoughts. I rang the bell. A pixie of a girl in baggy clothes opened the door and offered us tea, but insisted we wait there in the hallway and she would bring our drinks to us. Something did not feel right. After a few minutes, Bryan appeared. Expecting him to lead us to a room or office, we were somewhat taken aback when he said we would do the interview right there, in the hallway, three feet from his front door. It was patently clear we weren't welcome guests in his house. I told him of our earlier meeting through Lucy and he simply nodded as if that mattered little. I was starting to worry.

We set up cameras and microphones as best we could in the cramped space, and Bryan asked me what it was we actually wanted to talk to him about. I explained again that it was a simple question that in no way should offend him, but it was important that we asked only once the cameras were rolling. He nodded again. With everything in place, Bryan and I sat opposite each other on the doorstep. I told him the basic premise of the film, but his complete lack of reaction was scaring me, and I was stalling on the big question.

"As you know, people do make tribute albums to all kinds of artists, and we thought it would be a sweet and novel idea to travel around and talk to people like yourself and see if we could get a tribute album made to an unknown songwriter. It's never been done before."

Bryan was just looking at me with blatant disinterest. The tension in the room was becoming unbearable so I cut to it:

"Well, the question is, if we gave you a song of mine, would you, at least in principle, consider it?"

Bryan shook his head and said. "It would totally depend on the song."

Not as bad a response as I had feared, but he still looked distinctly unhappy.

"Of course," I said, "but if we gave you the song to listen to would you at least think about it?"

Bryan shook his head again. "I don't do that kind of thing very often because I write my own songs, you know."

In an effort to lighten the mood, I showed him the poster Mick had designed for the film.

Bryan chuckled and said, "That's sweet."

For a fleeting moment, I felt just a little easier.

Mick then asked Bryan, "Here's a question, have you been on a tribute album to anyone?"

"The only thing I've done like that is when I did a Chuck Berry song. But it was for charity. I only ever normally do these kinds of things for charity."

"This is for charity," I said. Bryan looked disappointed that his exit route had been blocked.

I continued anyway. "I have a CD here of the song…" but before I could finish my sentence, Bryan slapped the doorstep and said:

"Just drop it here, man."

There was no way he was touching that CD on camera. It really wasn't looking good, and my heart was slowly but surely sinking.

"I'll check it out," said Bryan, but with a grin that told me he would sooner throw it out.

It hadn't gone anything like as well as we had expected, but our job was done. We were dying to get out of there, but Bryan wasn't done with us.

"I think you'll find if you do this with other artists, they won't dig it. You should be honest with people right from the beginning."

We had been nothing but honest. We had made it very clear in the emails two weeks prior and in the conversation two minutes before the cameras rolled: there was a question that could only be asked on film. Even so, I assured him that no offence was intended and if he felt put out in anyway, I was deeply sorry, as that wasn't our intention.

Bryan wasn't accepting any apology.

"If I had known this was what you wanted to do, I would have probably said no. Not only that, but if you know Lucy and she knows what was going on here…"

Now I am torn. I am angry. All we have asked was if the man would consider being on a tribute album to an unknown songwriter if all the money went to a kid's music charity, and he was acting like we had set a trap for him using Lucy as bait. All he had to say was, 'I'll think about it' and later decline, but he seemed intent on putting us in our place. However, I am also straight-jacketed; if this back fires on Lucy and her friendship with him, I would find it hard to forgive myself.

He then gave Mick the darkest look of the day before turning to me and saying:

"You know it, though, you know it." He looked at me with nothing but disdain.

I tried to placate him by explaining that we thought that the idea was sweet enough that he couldn't possibly be offended by it, but Bryan was standing up and removing his microphone.

He said: "No, I'm not offended, but we'll wrap it up right there."

While we're hurriedly packing the equipment away, Bryan said:

"It's quite funny actually."

It was anything but funny to me.

A FAR CRY FROM SUNSET

Mike said: "There is a spirit behind it that we were hoping to capture."

"Well, you just might," says Bryan. "But I tell ya, you are going to meet publicists who are, like, from hell."

The cameras are now in the bag but one of them, oddly enough, is still running and capturing what slowly becomes a very dark conversation.

Bryan says: "As musician to musician, you should always be a straight shooter, and it's better to go through the right channels. You had better do it safe, you know. Lucy is a friend of mine."

His insistence that Lucy is his friend, as if she weren't mine, has me grinding my teeth. This is getting tough, but Bryan lectures on:

"I'm not giving you any new shit about it. Don't do this, man, you're never gonna get through the publicists."

Mick asks him, "If publicists are just gonna give us hell, what's the best move then?"

"Send the music, send a letter, and hope the music speaks for itself." is Bryan's advice.

Strange advice coming from a man who five minutes earlier wouldn't even touch the CD.

I try again to explain. "Look, this is a heartfelt thing, it's from the heart, all we're asking is would you like to help us out."

Now, Bryan is not even listening. He's just tearing us and our project apart.

"You bring me your CD with your song and it's like – why would I even wanna listen to it? After we've gone through this conversation, you think I'm gonna want to listen to *that*!?"

Now we really are trying to leave, but Bryan's fury thunders on:

"People are just gonna tell you to fuck off! You're crazy if you think that's gonna work out. No one is ever gonna do this. I mean, I may be wrong, and I wish you luck on your quest, but as a songwriter, me speaking, never.... won't happen."

OK, he wishes us luck, but he's never going to do it. Can we go now? It seems not.

"You know, I'm just gonna tell you what I think, and you're gonna take it! If we were in a bar, we'd be outside having a scrap."

I cannot exaggerate the absurdity of both the prospect of such a scrap, and the fact that his reaction has taken him to the point of suggesting one. He is still ranting.

"You know what I'm saying? Let's go outside and sort it out if you're gonna bullshit me. Nobody needs it, you know. You don't like it in your life, and I don't like it in mine."

Have you ever been caught in one of those pointless tirades where the other person has just lost it, and all you want to do is get the fuck out of there? Well, imagine that, but the other person is Bryan Adams.

At the first lull in his tirade, we scramble out of the front door. Outside, we take a few deep breaths before heading around the corner to the river wall to recover our balance. I try over and again to call Lucy to warn her of the storm heading her way, but her number is constantly busy. We know who has her attention, and we know the verbal onslaught the poor girl must be going through.

I eventually call her sister, Emma, who has spoken to Lucy briefly. She tells us Bryan has ripped Lucy apart something terrible; ranting furiously for 15 minutes; accusing her of setting him up and betraying their friendship. I feel rotten at my very heart. Lucy is a fine friend and I love the girl. Even though I can't be responsible for Bryan's insane tantrum, I feel I have instigated some terrible damage. We head back to my house. On my phone at home are three messages from Lucy. She is sobbing helplessly through all of them as she relays the tirade of insults and accusations Bryan had aimed at her. We sit for a few minutes afterwards in an awful, depressive silence.

Then, Mick says:

"My biggest disappointment in this whole thing, seriously, is that my daughter, Morgan, six years old, gave me this DVD for which Bryan Adams did the music. It's her favorite movie. She asked me to get it signed for her. But in the entire hubbub, I totally forgot. So...we're gonna have to go back!"

Our raucous laughter and genuine relief made my body shake and my eyes burn.

A FAR CRY FROM SUNSET

Alone With What You Know

(Scan QR code to download song)

10. The Strange Story of Myself

You're looking at a man whose dreams didn't come true.

Some dreams come from greed or vanity; your face on the cover of Rolling Stone; your arms full of Grammys; and your feet walking on red carpet. Many of my own dreams were no better than this, but I also had ambitions. These were made from more honorable yearnings. I wanted to be as good a songwriter as my own heroes, and I believe I have written songs that would make many of them proud. I wanted to make the stage my home and be able to talk from there as if surrounded by friends. I do that most weeks of my life. I wanted to travel the world and return home with incredible stories to tell. I believe you have read some right here.

I started from the lowest possible point. I was raised in the most extreme poverty by a single mother with a kind but badly broken heart. I had no formal education whatsoever. I have never once sat for an exam or composed an essay. For a long time, I believed that Jesus,

Romeo & Juliet, the dinosaurs, and Sherlock Holmes were all knocking around at the same time in the same place. I assumed Scotland and Russia were neighbors simply because both countries were cold. I was a shy and lonesome kid who spent his days walking alongside the River Thames dreaming of a life bigger, brighter, and less cruel than the one into which I was born. I was stubborn when it came to the truth. I wouldn't take anybody's word for anything.

I remember staying in a hostel with my mother and above my bed was a rusty one-bar fire wired to the light fitting. Before she went to sleep, she told me that if I touched the cable that hung above me I would get an electric shock and die. I lay on that bed for hours knowing it just could not be so. I could not sleep until I knew if I was being lied to. Eventually, I summoned the courage to reach up and grab it tightly in my fist. Nothing. I turned on my side and went peacefully to sleep. An old Irish woman once told me and my brother Jim that if you dropped the ace of spades under a table and you bent down to pick it up, you would see the devil. I went straight home and tried it. Either the devil was busy under someone else's table, or again I had overcome an unnecessary fear. I remember the day I was first told that if I pulled a face and the wind changed, it would stay that way. On the next windy day, I walked around for hours, pulling all the ugliest faces I could, and not once did I get stuck with any of them.

As a teenager, I pretty much locked myself in my bedroom and taught myself guitar and piano. In Fulham Court at that time, fighting and football were the more common pastimes. I wasn't particularly good at either of them. As soon as I had sought out friends who were interested in making music, I spent more and more of my time with them. The closest of these was, of course, Lee. That friendship deserves a book all to itself; from pushing that wheelchair around the streets of Fulham, to taking our one and only limo ride to LAX airport from The Hollywood Roosevelt Hotel in LA. It has been a story of music and a little burglary unlike any other. Lee has been at the helm while I made all of my solo records, and to the left of me on every stage I have trodden. We have seen the arrival of each other's children and the departure of each other's loved ones. I have a cassette at home of the two of us singing *All Shook Up* by Elvis from 1972. We finished recording my newest batch of songs just a few weeks ago, 38 years later.

In my twenties, I took up to four night classes a week and began my own education. I would walk to the library opposite Fulham Court every two or three days exchanging the maximum allowed five books for five new ones before returning home. I read everything.

History, art, psychology, even physics. I once read a four volume set entitled *Russian Revolutions 1901 to 1921* because I overheard a conversation about Lenin and it didn't sound as if he were one of The Beatles.

Learning became a joy, but most of all, I read literature. I devoured Steinbeck and Hemingway, Faulkner, Conrad and, best of all, Mark Twain. I read every novel and essay George Orwell ever wrote. Each book would lead me to another. These people conjured with words and made new worlds appear as if from nowhere. They wrote sentences that sent fireworks soaring through my mind and illuminated ideas of my own. But more than anything else, they taught me that I wasn't alone. And for that reason more than any other, I wanted to be like them. What their words did when put to paper I wanted mine to do when put to music.

In some ways, I was always talking back to that beaten little boy locked in a dark room at a foster home who was liberated from his misery by the sound of guitars, drums, and a velvet voice. If my own music could do half as much for any other lost soul, I would consider myself to have succeeded. It makes no difference if I call that a dream or an ambition, I believe I made it come true.

My mother died the same time The Faith Brothers ended. Her heart gave up in her sleep. A few months later, I tracked down my father in Ireland. To have done so while my mother was alive would have been hurtful to her. The final track on The Faith Brothers' *A Human Sound* CD, *A Boy & The River* tells the story of how my life felt in his absence. First I called a private detective and asked how much to track someone down. He quoted me 300 pounds. "Why so much?" I asked.

He then ran through the list of things he would have to do. I wrote them down and set about doing them myself. After making enquiries through the Salvation Army and the war pension's Records Office, my father and I eventually exchanged letters. I went to visit him in a little village just outside of Cork, Ireland. He has three beautiful daughters who adored him and did all they could to make me feel like family.

A FAR CRY FROM SUNSET

My father and I talked for days but had little in common. For all the questions asked and answers given, we could never be what we started out as. He could no longer be my father any more than I could now be his son. He died some years later while I was in America. I sat in Mick's back yard for some time trying to untangle my thoughts on his death, but it only ever felt like mourning the death of a stranger that I was supposed to have loved. That night, I sang for three hours straight in Merrifield's Bar, New Jersey, and I felt at peace. I'm glad that we had met. A mystery had been solved and a wound had been healed.

Since The Faith Brothers split in 1987, I have released five solo albums, and it is from these that the songs for *Tribute This!* were chosen. Only the first of these, *Mass*, did I ever take to a record company.

IRS Records was owned by the manager of The Police, Miles Copeland, and run by music industry wide-boy Steve Tannet. Within weeks of The Faith Brothers parting company, Tannet asked me to visit him at his office. I played him some early demos from *Mass*, and he liked them enough to release the album when it was ready. He asked me what I wanted in return. I took a guess at 10 grand. The album would have upwards of thirty musicians on it. Gospel singers, a string quartet, a brass section, even a full-sized, heavenly-sounding harp. I told him I could get all the players to take part on a deferred payment basis.

When the album was done, IRS would release it, and hand over the 10 grand so I could pay the musicians, the studio and the engineers. He agreed. The album was a full year in the making, and I always kept IRS updated on its progress. When it was finally finished, a meeting was arranged. Miles Copeland himself, along with all the IRS staff, would be there to hear the finished product. A room full of us sat through the 10 songs and when it was over, everyone in the room applauded. Tannet looked over at me.

"It's a beautiful record," he said. "we should get it on the shelves as soon as possible while The Faith Brothers are still on people's minds. There's only one problem. There is no 10 grand. IRS will put it out, but we can't give you any money for it."

He looked over at Miles Copeland who simply shook his head in agreement.

I was for a moment, simply stupefied. I looked at them both for a good few minutes before I got up, walked over to the cassette player, ejected my tape, and slipped it in my pocket. When I got to the door, I turned to Tannet.

"You lied to me," I said.

Then I closed the door behind me.

I eventually borrowed enough money from a loan shark to take care of the very few musicians who insisted on being paid and pressed the CD myself. The return on the loan was five grand, and I had to play as many as six bars a week singing covers for three years before the debt was cleared.

A FAR CRY FROM SUNSET

I have never again since approached a record company with an album of mine.

Halfway through recording my last album, *The Turtledove Boutique*, we felt yet another death of someone we loved; our friend and drummer for the last decade, Nigel Hammond. He and his wife had taken a long weekend break in Scotland. Their dog had fallen into the fast-moving River Spey. Both he and his wife jumped in to pull the dog out but the current was too strong. Nigel's wife, Lisa, and the dog were saved by wedding guests who had heard Lisa's screaming from where they stood on the steps of a nearby church. Lisa and the dog were pulled to safety after half an hour of struggling to stay afloat. Poor Nigel's washed up body was found miles downstream an hour later. Once again, I would sing at the funeral of a friend. This time, The Faith Brothers' *A Different Kind Of Wonderful* was the song. It was Nigel's favorite, and reflected beautifully how Lee and I thought of him.

I have an old friend named Ron. He, like Lee's dad, Dave, is the father of friends of mine, Sue and Jeanette, who are both married to Lee's brothers, Mark and Tim. Ron has encouraged and supported me from the very beginning. When I was awful, he said I wasn't bad, when I wasn't bad, he persuaded me I was good and when I got good, he assured me I was great.

He's been coming to shows as long as I have been playing them, and always enjoys the songs as if he were hearing them for the first time. Anyway, when my brother Jim died, Ron said the kindest thing one man could ever say about another: He said Jim made you feel that running into you was the best thing that had happened to him that day. Well, Jim and Nigel had more than playing the drums in common. Nigel could quite easily make you feel the same way.

♦

When we started our travels to make *Tribute This!*, I did feel a little like the kid in *The Wizard of Oz*. I had three friends who just wanted to help make something come good for me. And as with the so many journeys of discovery, what we had sought out could never compare to what we had learned about ourselves and the world around us in trying to get there. There were times when I felt our lives were being lived so brilliantly that I could not imagine it was ever that good for the artists we were seeking. They seemed cut off and protected, hidden away and sheltered by comparison. I remember a single, shining thought that came to me time and time again as we made our way around the world. Right now, I thought, I wouldn't take one year of their lives in exchange for one day of the life we were living.

In complete contrast for over a decade, and all through the making of our film, a guy who is probably more globally known than any of them has treated me as a confidante, an equal and a friend.

I was stuffing my battered acoustic guitar into its equally ragged case when Simon, my good friend and owner and raconteur of The Troubadour, stopped me and asked if I would be happy to stay after hours and entertain a small private party. He knows there's only one answer so we sit and wait for the last customers to leave and the staff to clean up. First into the basement club are two plain clothes security guards. One of them asks the head bartender about cameras. I see Bobby shake his head. He passes word to the guard behind him who beckons to a small crowd at the top of the stairs. They're young, in an upbeat mood but nothing rowdy. In the centre walks a kid with a baseball cap on but even without the visible red mop, there's no mistaking who the fuss is about. It's Prince Harry. He comes over, thanks me for staying, and asks what I'm drinking. Brandy, straight, no ice.

For the next three hours I sing my way through just about every tune I know. And Harry and the gang tear into every chorus with some gusto. Harry spends the whole night next to me shouting, whenever my glass looks empty, "Somebody get Billy a drink!" I take everyone as I find them and the kid, (he was only 18 at the time) is very cool and sweet. So much so that when I deliberately keep calling him the wrong name: Henry, Howard, Hughie and so on, he laughs louder than anyone else at the table. Even when I ask, "Sorry, Humphrey, what is it that you do again?". He is not the least bit offended.

All sung out and tired, we all head our separate ways. We have a hug at the top of the stairs and he jumps into a Jeep while I take the walk home. About two streets from my house, I stop, think about it, smile, think about it again and burst out laughing.

A few weeks went by and one Friday evening, I got a call from Simon. Harry was out and about and asked if Simon could get me out for another session. I was, at this time, spending most nights at the Troubadour and, with it being within staggering distance of my home, I was always ready for a night of good brandy and great song. So, royal or otherwise, it was always a joy to belt out some of my favorite songs to a party of revelers.

Soon it became a regular thing. At least once every few weeks, Harry would bring a gang down and I would get the call.

Then one morning, I got a strange text message. "Mate, sorry if things got a little rowdy last night, I think I may have bundled you and your girlfriend into the pile of rubbish outside the club." It wasn't signed so I replied.

"No need to apologize, if anyone fell into the rubbish it certainly wasn't me and my girl. By the way, who the fuck is this?" The reply came back. "H.Wales, your singing partner!"

I hadn't given him my number but the fact that he'd sought it out to apologize for a misdemeanor I had no part, in struck me as not only thoughtful, but also a sign of trust. I had his number.

A few days later, I was playing in an Irish bar in Earls Court. Halfway through the first set, I see guys who I now know pretty well. Harry's guards come in and station themselves in strategic parts of the room. Then in strolls Harry and sits right in front of me, all alone for the next hour or so.

Soon he and his friends were coming to all my shows, big and small. Highlighting with a packed house at London's famous Shepherds Bush Empire. It was my birthday and we all went back to the Troubadour after the show to celebrate.

A FAR CRY FROM SUNSET

I don't think it would be disingenuous to say that by now we considered ourselves friends, often texting and meeting for beers at various parties.

One night, after a quiet drink at the Troubadour, I took a refreshing walk home. I got myself cleaned up and was just about to fall into bed when the phone rang. It was Harry. Tomorrow was the 10th anniversary of his mother's death. He had a speech to make and from what I could tell, he was worried that what he had written was maybe too informal. He told me a little about it and all I could tell him was: "Harry, you're a good guy, you've got a big heart, anything you say that's true to you could never be wrong." He thanked me and I sat on the edge of my bed and allowed myself a grin.

A couple of summers ago, I went with Harry and a bunch of his pals to see The Killers at Hyde Park. As I left Hyde Park Station and began to stroll through the park, a fleet of Jeeps drove slowly by. One of them stopped, down went the tinted window and out popped the head of my red-headed friend. "Come on mate, jump in."

I climb in the back and we are whisked to the back-stage area. We have a few drinks but I have to leave to play a friend's wedding in Slough, I won't get to see The Killers.

When the wedding gig was done I got a call from Marco, Harry's close friend and mentor,

"Grab your guitar and get to the Troubadour as soon as you can, mate. I've got an audience for you."

For the next three hours I sat at a table and sang. On my left was Tom Jones (we duetted on *It's Not Unusual*), next to him, Natalie Imbruglia, next to her, The Killers and finally the third in line to the throne, Prince Harry.

I met the older brother, William a few times too and he proved to be equally courteous and fun.

The first time we met, Harry had brought him along for one of our late night sessions at The Troubadour. As I ushered him through the side door into a private room he exclaimed,

"Oh, so you're the famous Billy?"

"Well, my name is actually William, but ever since people started making a royal fuss about the name, I had to shorten it to Billy."

"I like you already," he said, "let's get some shots!" For a few months, he too would come for the late night sessions and, like his brother, always treated me with kindness and respect.

He once picked me up from under my arms and swung me round in circles while shouting out my name real loud. Surreal.

During this time the brothers asked for my band and I to play at the launch of a charity they had started in the name of a colleague who had lost his life in Afghanistan.

A FAR CRY FROM SUNSET

Now picture this. The official bash is over. Its 2:00 am, the band is still kicking and the place is still jumping. William walks to the stage and asks if he can duet with me on the *Oasis* song, *Don't Look Back in Anger.* We share a microphone and I agree to jump in whenever he forgets the words.

He's quite drunk. His eyes are crossed as he tries to focus on the microphone. His voice has taken on a gentle slur. For a moment I want to laugh. Then he looks straight at me and his face lights up with real joy.

The thought occurs to me that moments of pure abandonment like this are scarce for a young man so closely watched at every turn. I smile back simply because I am moved by his obvious happiness.

That moment still twinkles at the back of my mind whenever I see him on the news at so many formal occasions.

I am jolted from the moment by a sudden burst of percussive chaos. I turn to see what's going on behind me. It's Harry, leaning over the drum kit furiously tweaking the drummer's nipples, making it impossible for him to keep time. William and I both crack up with laughter. Soon the whole room is roaring.

At the end of the night William introduced me to his then girlfriend, Kate, in a way that made me smile broadly. "Have you met Billy? The man's an absolute legend." She gets up from her seat, shakes my one hand with both of hers, kisses both my cheeks and thanks me for indulging William at the microphone.

Like so many times in my life, I found myself asking, "how did *I* get *here*?"

In the summer of 2010, I put out a record and donated all the funds to Harry's African charity for orphans in Lesotho. During this time, a Russian vodka company offered me 30,000 pounds to put on a show in their tent at a polo tournament, but only if I could bring Harry along. I turned them down flat. When I told Harry, he said:

"You knob-head! I would have turned up for 10 minutes, had my picture taken and you could have make 30 grand."

"Harry," I said, "it's a bad principle and simply not my style."

He, unlike some of the artists we had talked to, had no issue at all with doing anything that might give me a hand up.

♦

But if there was a wizard at the end of our yellow brick road, it was the final artist on our list; the songwriter for whom my admiration is boundless. A man whose songwriting canon, with the possible exception of Cole Porter, outguns everyone before and after him in popular music: Sir Paul McCartney.

I was back at home in London and gigging the pubs and clubs with my band. Mike, Mick and Gary were back in Philadelphia. They were going to put the same question to Paul McCartney that we had taken to all the other artists by road, rail, and flight for almost a year, but they would do so by the only means left available to them. They were going to write him a letter. With time and money having both long run out, all they could afford to do was write him a letter, print it out on a computer, and send it to him. I wasn't there when they composed it, but they later sent me the film they had shot while doing so. It was a final beautiful gesture from three beautiful friends with whom I had shared the greatest of all adventures. And it brought me to tears.

Dear Sir Paul,

It is with wishful sentiment that we write this letter. So it was almost two years ago we set out on a quest in an attempt to give something back to a friend who has given us, and many others, so much over the years. This friend, Billy Franks, is a singer/songwriter who has practiced his craft for over thirty years. His dedication to his music has kept him doing it all that time, despite no real recognition.

So, our mission. Our mission is to ask ten famous singer/songwriters to appear on a tribute album to Billy Franks, an unknown but worthy subject of such an honor. Our trek has taken us to five countries and spans almost two hundred thousand miles in scope. We've experienced many ups and downs along the way, but we were guided by Billy's music and his devotion to his craft.

Every time we hear one of Billy's songs or watch him perform, we are reminded not of our quest, but of his personal voyage. Billy Franks has pursued his dream for three decades, and has not wavered in his resolve to produce only the best material. His pursuit of his dream has been the most inspiring thing to us.

When people hear what we're doing, they're impressed with our resolve and our dedication to our friend. But what they don't understand is that his voyage started over three decades ago in a London housing project. Our devotion to Billy is nothing compared to his devotion to his craft.

Throughout the past year we knew the chance of us achieving our goal was improbable, if not impossible, but we persisted. But why not persist? Did Billy give up when he was told the world would never hear his music? Did Billy give up when those around him were leaving the music behind in search of some real work? Did Billy give up when he was homeless with nothing but his guitar and his music?

So Paul, you're our final hope. We knew that if we could persuade you to appear on a tribute to our friend, then many of the other artists would follow suit.

We have reached the end of our journey but, regardless of the outcome, we have achieved the ultimate success. By attempting this quest together, we have fortified a friendship and affirmed the love and respect for the music of someone we love.

And we did it all in the name of our friend's dream. Imagine a greater tribute than that.

The End

A FAR CRY FROM SUNSET

The Strange Story of Myself

(Scan QR code to download song)

BILLY FRANKS

EPILOGUE

In the winter after filming was finished, my three friends and I hired an isolated cabin high in the Poconos Mountains just outside of Philadelphia. There, surrounded by 4 feet of snow, we hunkered down for more than a week, the four of us worked tirelessly, trying to hone a 90-minute feature documentary from more than 200 hours of footage. With a finished edit in hand, we toured the U.S. independent film circuit with *Tribute This!* bringing audiences to their feet and picking up a string of awards. Suitably encouraged, we sent copies to the managers, publicists and record labels of all 10 artists featured in the film. Included with each DVD was an open-hearted letter telling of our adventures and asking if their charges could be persuaded to take their place on the tribute album.

We never received a single reply.

I am neither surprised nor hurt by this. I have the comfort of knowing not one of the 10 could ever have as beautiful a portrait of themselves as the one my friends had fashioned in film for me.

Billy

Now Enjoy The Movie

(Scan QR code to download movie)

A FAR CRY FROM SUNSET

ABOUT THE AUTHOR

Billy Franks was singer/songwriter for The Faith Brothers who released two albums and six singles with Siren/Virgin records in the mid-80s. Billy then went on to release six solo CDs.

In the summer of 2010, Billy released a single, *The Beautiful Game,* to help raise money and awareness for Prince Harry's African charity, Sentebale.

2012 saw the release of his 7th solo CD, From The Court To The Empire, recorded 'live' at London's landmark venue, The Shepherds Bush Empire.

Billy's brand new album 'A Letter to The Times' is now available to download from iTunes, Spotify, Google Play etc. You can also get a copy of the CD plus other exclusives from:
www.billyfranks.com

Thank you, John Mullan, Caroline McIntosh, Sharon Williams, Glyn Hughes & The Sweet Family AKA " the Partridges "

Printed in Great Britain
by Amazon